Foot
Tou

with Ken Ward

North York
Moors

. . . a marvellous freedom from the tumult of the world

St Aeldred

Abbot of Rievaulx
(Twelfth century)

This new *Footpath-Touring* route pioneered by Ken Ward is
a lovely walk, embracing much of the best of the moors.
It will cause you to discover superb scenery, absorbing
historical and archaeological features, and dream-like villages.

Harry Mead
(author of *Inside the North York Moors*)

Jarrold Colour Publications, Norwich

About *Footpath-Touring*

This *Footpath-Touring* guide is designed to lead you easily along a wonderful walk to show you the best of the North Yorkshire Moors.

The route: The tour has been divided into short daily stages that are well within the capabilities of those quite new to walking. More experienced walkers will, of course, extend these stages as they wish.

Accommodation: Panels on the maps give advice on overnight accommodation in three price categories: economy, medium and not cheap. All provide reasonable value, while some are outstandingly good. It is wise to check costs when making reservations.

Unless indicated, all will provide an evening meal. I suggest that when booking you make it quite clear if a meal is required, and, if possible, give some idea of your anticipated time of arrival. Where the accommodation is a pub or is licensed to sell alcohol, this is indicated.

Where possible, locations are indicated on the maps. Telephone numbers are always given, should further directions be necessary.

Two letters after the name show the period that accommodation is usually available; for example, A/O = April to October, M/N = March to November. Those open all year are identified with a □; however, remember that during winter months the owners may be decorating, taking holidays, or repairing burst water-pipes!

Out of season it should be sufficient to make a telephone reservation the day before. This gives you great flexibility in your tour programme, allowing you to take non-walking days to suit inclinations and weather. At busier times, reservations should be made as early as possible.

All the accommodation has been selected for the proprietors' appreciation of the needs of *Footpath-Touring* walkers, particularly regarding warm rooms, good food, drying facilities, early starts and substantial packed lunches. Those places where I have received a particularly warm welcome are outlined in green. All the places indicated have become known to me during research for the tour. I offer them in good faith, without accepting responsibility for them. However I will always be grateful to receive, via the publisher, any comments you may wish to make.

Please mention *Footpath-Touring* when making reservations, as all accommodations have been asked to suggest alternatives should they be fully booked.

Footwear: I consider it essential to wear walking boots when *Footpath-Touring* in the North York Moors. A few of the bridleway sections are well churned-up by horse traffic, and consequently very muddy in wet periods, especially in those places hidden from the sun by trees. Boots will give the necessary ankle-support when walking through heather and on stony paths, and cleated soles will provide a good grip and cushion the soles of the feet. Seek the advice of a reputable local outdoor shop, select comfortable, lightweight walking boots and wear them as much as possible before you begin your *Footpath-Touring* holiday. These boots are your wheels and you carry no spare – so choose wisely.

Waterproofs: Assume that there will be wet days. However rain is no hardship if you are properly protected. A lightweight waterproof jacket with hood, pockets and front opening and lightweight waterproof over-trousers that can easily be slipped over booted feet are essential. Lightweight gaiters are available that go from boot to knee, and these are useful on all but the driest days. Even when there is no rain, they will protect trouser-legs from dew-laden grass or bridleway mud.

Non-walking days: If poor weather or other reasons suggest that you should take a non-walking day, the next overnight stop can always be reached by taxi, and telephone numbers of conveniently located operators are included on the maps. Always check the fare first, and mention *Footpath-Touring* to benefit from any advantageous rates. Similarly, local bus-service details are included at various stages.

About *Footpath-Touring*

Luxury *Footpath-Touring*: For a holiday of real luxury, let someone else carry your baggage! Telephone numbers of reliable taxi operators are given throughout the route. (Mention *Footpath-Touring!*) These will transfer your luggage to your next port of call, leaving you to carry only a small day-sack with a few walking essentials. Much recommended.

Maps: The maps in the guide, together with the accompanying directions, allow you to follow the route easily. However I strongly suggest that you equip yourself with the excellent one-inch Ordnance Survey Tourist Map, *North York Moors,* which covers the whole tour. This will enable you to identify distant features, allow you to make your own diversions, and greatly add to your tour.

Guardian Angels: On some of the maps you will see reference to Guardian Angels. Should a situation develop during a day when a telephone call becomes essential, and there are no public telephones in the vicinity, you may call on these kindly Angels for help. They are all volunteers, of course, and any calls made should be paid for.

Good behaviour: Please behave in a responsible and thoughtful manner during your Footpath Tour. Be careful about closing gates, keeping dogs under proper control – and please – no litter!

This North York Moors Tour

You can complete this *Footpath-Touring* holiday in a week of easy walking, so that your programme might look like this:

> *Friday:* travel to Danby (see page 4). Commence tour on *Saturday* and walk every day, to arrive at Goathland on following *Sunday* and travel home.

However, if you have extra days to spare, you could take the North York Moors Railway down to Pickering from Levisham on the seventh day. Pickering has castle remains, interesting wall paintings in the church, Isle Beck Museum of Rural Life, shops and good hotels and pubs. The tour can be further extended by walking from Goathland, via delightful Beck Hole, to Grosmont along the disused railway track. The *Historical Railway Trail,* published by the North York Moors National Park, is an excellent, low-priced guidebook for the route. Details of transport and taxis allow you to complete the tour as a series of expeditions or long week-ends.

Footpath-Touring – An Introduction

You are strongly advised to read the 32-page book, *Footpath-Touring – An Introduction.* This gives a great deal of useful advice, based on many years' experience of *Footpath-Touring* throughout the British Isles. It shows how baggage can be kept to the sensible and comfortable weight of about 11 lb *5 kg* for men and 10 lb *4.5 kg* for women. Advice is given on choosing walking clothing which will ensure comfort and safety, together with suggestions for lightweight evening wear; kit checklists are included for both men and women. Hints are given on selecting a pack which will carry the load comfortably and efficiently. Other sections deal with medical kits, foot-care, choice of footwear, wet-weather clothing, necessities and luxuries. A chapter gives a brief history of the footpath system in Britain; how it has evolved over the centuries, and how it is now protected by law. Finally, advice is given on making the most efficient use of the *Footpath-Touring* guidebooks, and how to ensure a successful and rewarding tour. A most useful acquisition! Available from good booksellers for the low price of £1; or from the publishers for £1.26, including post and packing:

Jarrold Colour Publications, Barrack Street, Norwich NR3 1TR *or*
Footpath-Touring, The Manor, Moreton Pinkney, Daventry NN11 6SJ

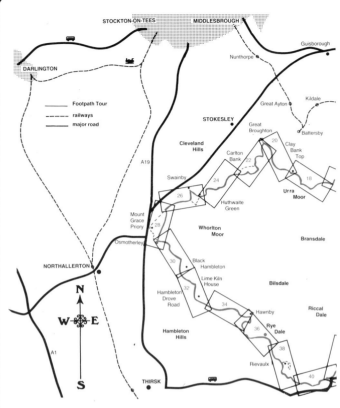

Getting to Danby

By rail: To Middlesbrough via Darlington, then by the British Rail Esk Valley line, which runs between Middlesbrough and Whitby. A delightful scenic journey on a rare surviving 'rural branch line'. The journey to Danby, one of fifteen stations, takes approximately 45 minutes.

Six trains a day, Monday to Saturday, from 07.20 to 18.15; Sundays, May to October only, four trains from 09.35 to 16.00.

Enquiries: *Telephone: 0642 225535.* (Overseas enquiries: British Rail, Zetland Road, Middlesbrough, TS1 1EG.)

By coach/rail: To Middlesbrough by National Express. Enquiries: *0325 468771.* (Overseas enquiries: United Automobile Services, Feethams Bus Station, Darlington, Co. Durham.)

Then by train to Danby as above.

By car/rail: Cars may be parked for the duration of your Footpath Tour at the British Rail manned car park at Whitby for approximately 50p a day. (Park close to car park attendant's hut and mention *Footpath-Touring*.)

Then by Esk Valley line for the 30-minute journey to Danby. Six trains a day, Monday to Saturday, from 09.22 to 19.56; Sunday, May to October only, four trains from 11.40 to 17.52.

Enquiries: As rail above.

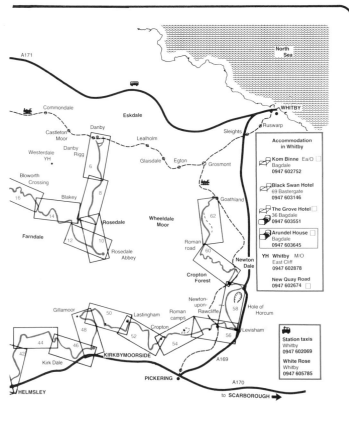

From Goathland

By rail: The North Yorkshire Moors Railway runs trains (most of them steam-hauled) on the 15-minute journey from Goathland to Grosmont every day from March to October. Enquiries: *0751 72508*.

Then by Esk Valley line for the 75-minute journey to Middlesbrough.

Six trains a day, Monday to Saturday, from 09.38 to 20.12; Sunday, May to October only, from 11.56 to 18.08.

Enquiries: As rail opposite.

Walking: To Grosmont. The North Yorkshire Moors National Park publishes an excellent guide, *Historical Railway Trail*, to a well-maintained walk along the track bed of the original railway, opened in 1836. Takes about 1½ hours of very pleasant walking. Recommend that you include the small detour to the hamlet of Beck Hole.

Then by Esk Valley line as above.

By bus/rail: To Whitby. A frequent service from Easter to October every day. Four buses a day only, October to Easter, and one only on Sunday at 17.31. Enquiries: *0904 624161*.

Then by Esk Valley line for the 90-minute journey to Middlesbrough. Enquiries as rail opposite.

By car: Return to Whitby as above.

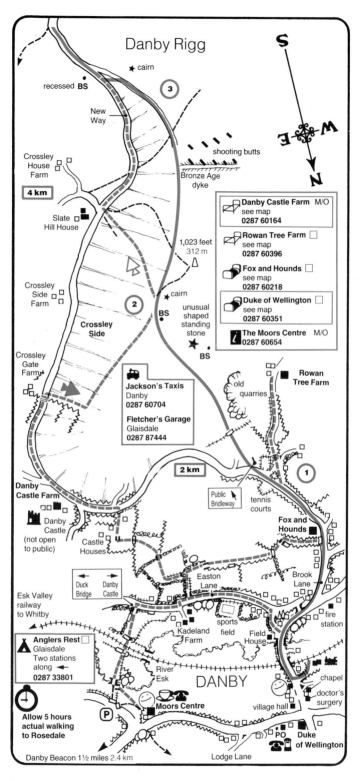

Danby Rigg

★ cairn

recessed **BS**

New Way

shooting butts

Crossley House Farm

Bronze Age dyke

4 km

Slate Hill House

1,023 feet 312 m

Crossley Side Farm

★ cairn

BS

unusual shaped standing stone

Crossley Side

BS

Crossley Gate Farm

Danby Castle Farm M/O
see map
0287 60164

Rowan Tree Farm ☐
see map
0287 60396

Fox and Hounds ☐
see map
0287 60218

Duke of Wellington ☐
see map
0287 60351

The Moors Centre M/O
0287 60654

old quarries

Rowan Tree Farm

Jackson's Taxis
Danby
0287 60704

Fletcher's Garage
Glaisdale
0287 87444

2 km

Public Bridleway

tennis courts

Danby Castle Farm

Fox and Hounds

Danby Castle
(not open to public)

Castle Houses

Easton Lane

Brook Lane

←Duck Bridge Danby Castle→

Esk Valley railway to Whitby

Kadeland Farm

sports field

Field House

fire station

Anglers Rest ☐
Glaisdale
Two stations along ←
0287 33801

River Esk

DANBY

chapel

doctor's surgery

Allow 5 hours actual walking to Rosedale

Moors Centre

village hall

PO

Duke of Wellington

Lodge Lane

Danby Beacon 1½ miles 2.4 km

Lunch: Remote moorland walking means a packed lunch will be needed. Down on a grassed-over railway track there are ideal spots for a picnic with fine views of Rosedale.

Danby to Danby Rigg

Going: The route leads immediately up onto wild, exposed and historic moorland. However an initial diversion to the National Park Moors Centre is strongly recommended. Only a mile *1.6 km* to the east (a route is indicated on the map), the Centre, with its small exhibition and shop, makes an excellent introduction to this Footpath Tour. Refreshments. *Open daily, May to October: 10.00–18.00 hrs; February to April, November – weekends only. Small admission charge.*

Leave Danby railway station, turn Right on road to cross railway and river bridges.

Moors Centre diversion: just beyond river bridge and Field House, turn up Left, and Left into Easton Lane. Beyond Kadeland Farm, turn Left over stile and follow hedge on Right to cross railway – with great care! Continue over river bridge, over stile on Left and cross wild-flower meadow and picnic area to Moors Centre. Once the home of Canon Atkinson, who despite parish duties, three wives and thirteen children, wrote the classic, Forty years in a Moorland Parish.

For return, walk back to Easton Lane and leave by stile on Left just past Kadeland Farm. Where Danby Castle path goes Left, turn Right and follow field path to emerge on road near Fox and Hounds. Very little remains of Danby Castle (not open to public, but accommodation in farmhouse remains of SW tower). Thought to have been built in the fourteenth century by William le Latimer, relation of Henry VIII's widow, Katherine Parr.

Near fire station, fork Left into Brook Lane and up past Fox and Hounds.

On the green opposite the pub are covers protecting the clay squares used in the local game of quoits. Saucer-shaped iron quoits weighing just over five pounds *2 kg* are pitched about eight yards *7 m* to drop over the pin – or cunningly thrown to prevent rival players from doing so. Some say that the game was brought back by soldiers after Agincourt. Others blame the Romans!

Just past tennis courts, take signposted bridleway Right and follow multi-tracks up to fence and through gate. Continue this line on clear track through bracken and heather.

Note the six-foot-high *2 m* pentagon-shaped standing stone – all that remains of a 42-foot-diameter *13 m* Bronze Age stone circle.

At top edge of steep Crossley Side, right-of-way drops down to Slate Hill House, where turn Right to ascend New Way road. However a much better route is to continue along the edge of the ridge avoiding a loss of height and subsequent road climb. This is not a right-of-way, but landowners, Wykeham Estates, have kindly given approval for *Footpath-Touring* users to follow this route, *except on the rare occasions when grouse shooting is seen to be taking place from the butts near the path.* At line of butts, route becomes vehicle tracks. Where tracks join New Way road, it is usually boggy, so take thin path down to Left just a few yards before and join road at boundary stone.

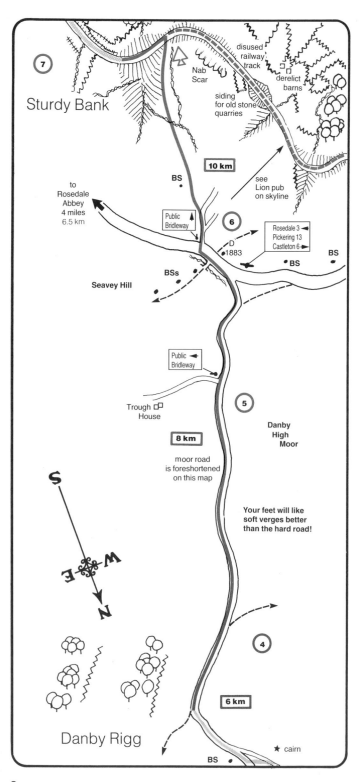

7

Sturdy Bank

disused railway track

Nab Scar

derelict barns

siding for old stone quarries

10 km

BS

see Lion pub on skyline

to Rosedale Abbey 4 miles 6.5 km

Public Bridleway

6

Rosedale 3
Pickering 13
Castleton 6

D 1883

BS

BS

BSs

Seavey Hill

Public Bridleway

Trough House

5

Danby High Moor

8 km

moor road is foreshortened on this map

Your feet will like soft verges better than the hard road!

S
W
E
N

4

6 km

Danby Rigg

★ cairn

BS

8

Danby Rigg to Sturdy Bank

Going: An easy route along a usually empty moorland road, then through heather down into Rosedale and a scenic, level walk along a disused, grass-covered railway track.

High on Danby Rigg, Bronze Age man left almost 800 piles of stones; some burial cairns and funerary circles, but mainly stone-clearance heaps to allow cultivation and grazing. *Rygg* is modern Norwegian for long narrow hill. If conditions are clear, see behind you, eleven miles *18 km* to the north-west, the distinctive cone of Roseberry Topping, at 1,052 feet *320 m*. Two miles *3 km* nearer stands the obelisk on Easby Moor commemorating local mariner and explorer, Captain Cook. Over to the west, ten miles *16 km* away, is the 930-foot *284 m* transmitter mast on Bilsdale Moor.

Continue up road for about two miles *3 km* to the Rosedale Abbey–Castleton road, where turn Left. In about 80 yards *73 m*, turn Right onto signposted bridleway. In a few yards, take Left fork. A little further on, where track bears Right, take thin track through heather to Left. After about ten minutes, a stream crosses the track and a chasm begins to form on the Left. Path now drops steeply down to wide grass embankment, once the route of a railway serving Rosedale East iron-ore mines.

It is now decision time. Turn to the Left, and within two hours (four easy miles *6.5 km*) you will be in Rosedale Abbey, with its friendly accommodation. On the other hand, by turning to the Right, you can be cosily in the historic Lion Inn on Blakey within one easy hour (two and half miles *4 km*). This latter choice has another advantage! The route from Rosedale Abbey to Great Broughton is fifteen and half miles *25 km* long. Despite eight miles *13 km* being easy and level, it still means about seven hours of actual walking. The Blakey option reduces this by four miles *6 km,* or about two hours!

Route to Rosedale Abbey:

Turn Left along the railway track for two miles *3 km,* with magnificent scenery looking down the dale. *Note that this is not officially designated a right-of-way, but landowners, Milburn Estates, have kindly given permission for it to be included in this* Footpath-Touring *route, with the reasonable request that dogs be kept under control, and walkers keep to the tramway.*

This line was opened by North Eastern Railway, on 18 August 1865, to run from a junction near the Blakey Lion for four and three-quarter miles *7.6 km* to Rosedale East ironstone mines. These mines actually began working in about 1859, with nine-foot-high *3 m* horizontal drifts driven deep into the valley side. A year after the railway was opened, over 168,000 tons of ironstone were produced, a figure doubled in the 1870s. The fascinating story of the mines and railway is given in *A History of Rosedale* by Raymond Hayes, published by the Moors National Park.

Direct route to Lion Inn:

Turn Right to follow the railway track easily around the dale-head, where impressive embankments cross Reeking Gill and the headwaters of the River Seven. Just past brick ruins which once supported a water tank, see the red roof of High Blakey House up on the Right, and follow thin path up through heather to boundary fencing. (See map, page 14.)

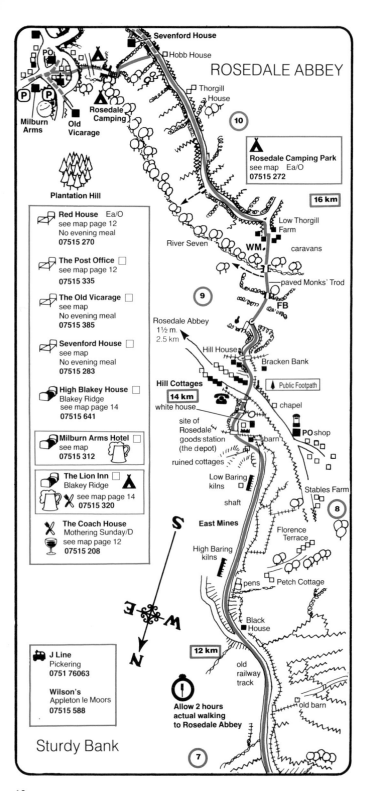

ROSEDALE ABBEY

Sevenford House
Hobb House
Thorgill House

(10)

▲ Rosedale Camping Park
see map Ea/O
07515 272

16 km

Low Thorgill Farm
WM.
caravans
River Seven
paved Monks' Trod

(9)

FB

Rosedale Abbey
1½ m.
2.5 km

Hill House
Bracken Bank

Hill Cottages

14 km
☎

white house
↑ Public Footpath

chapel

site of Rosedale goods station (the depot)

barn

PO shop
ruined cottages

Low Baring kilns

Stables Farm

shaft

(8)

East Mines
Florence Terrace

High Baring kilns
pens
Petch Cottage

Black House

12 km

old railway track

old barn

Sturdy Bank

(7)

PO
P
P

Milburn Arms

Old Vicarage

▲ Rosedale Camping

Plantation Hill

Red House Ea/O
see map page 12
No evening meal
07515 270

The Post Office □
see map page 12
07515 335

The Old Vicarage □
see map
No evening meal
07515 385

Sevenford House □
see map
No evening meal
07515 283

High Blakey House □
Blakey Ridge
see map page 14
07515 641

Milburn Arms Hotel □
see map
07515 312

The Lion Inn □ ▲
Blakey Ridge
see map page 14
07515 320

The Coach House
Mothering Sunday/D
see map page 12
07515 208

J Line
Pickering
0751 76063

Wilson's
Appleton le Moors
07515 588

S
E ✦ W
N

Allow 2 hours actual walking to Rosedale Abbey

Sturdy Bank to Rosedale Abbey

Going: An easy two-mile *3 km* walk along the level, grass-covered, disused railway track is followed by a short field footpath and a length of quiet lane into Rosedale Abbey.

Continue on the railway track past the remains of Black House on the Right – an old linesman's cottage – and past the siding, Left, which once took the line up to the mine workings.

On the horizon on the Right across the dale, see the twin pillars which are all that is left of another iron mine – Sheriff's Pit.

Pass ruin of High Baring kilns on Left.

This towering masonry, looking a little like something in the Luxor Valley, is all that remains of three large calcining kilns, where the ore was tipped into the top to be 'roasted' to drive off water and carbonic acid gas and reduce the weight – not only to cut down transport costs, but also to keep down the royalties of 6d per ton due to the estate! In half a mile *80 m* are the remains of the earlier sixteen kilns of Low Baring with, above, the squat, square chimney which served as a ventilator. The mines continued to be profitably worked up to the end of the 1914–18 war, but then a familiar story took over. Increasing costs and the appearance of low-cost foreign ore sounded warnings. The mine was closed during the General Strike of 1926 and never reopened.

In a quarter of a mile *40 m,* pass ruined cottages on Left, and bear Left with barn on Right – once store-shed of the old Rosedale goods station. Make your way across boggy debris and through gate onto sunken lane. Pass, on Right, old coal bunkers and white Depot Cottage – and duck pond!

Down at Hill Cottages, cross road into lane past Bracken Bank and Hill House and lock-up garages. Continue down lane, through two kiss-gates to turn Right in field by waymark post. Follow paved Monks' Trod down through two hedges to stile and footbridge over River Seven. Up through caravan site to Low Thorgill Farm.

Monks' Trod is one of the paths of single paving stones said to have been laid by monks or Quakers to ease progress of pack-horses. Trade and distribution on the moors in the Middle Ages relied heavily on these lines of ponies, which carried loads in 'wackas', or panniers, in trains that could consist of 40–50 animals. Even as late as 1880, moor coal was still carried to lime kilns at Hutton-le Hole and Cropton by pack-horses.

Through Low Thorgill Farm turn Left on road. In just over ten minutes take second signposted footpath on Left to follow another ancient paved path down to trees to re-cross river at steps and footbridge. Follow signposted path through campsite into Rosedale Abbey.

Despite its name there never was an abbey here. In the fourteenth century a priory of the Cistercian order was established with nine nuns, a prioress and several *conversi* (lay workers). After the Dissolution, in July 1538, the cloisters were converted into cottages, the restored chancel became the parish church and the *conversi* buildings became, first the manor-house, and now the Milburn Arms. A small part of a belfry with a stone spiral staircase still stands – but that only just. (See it after leaving the caravan park.)

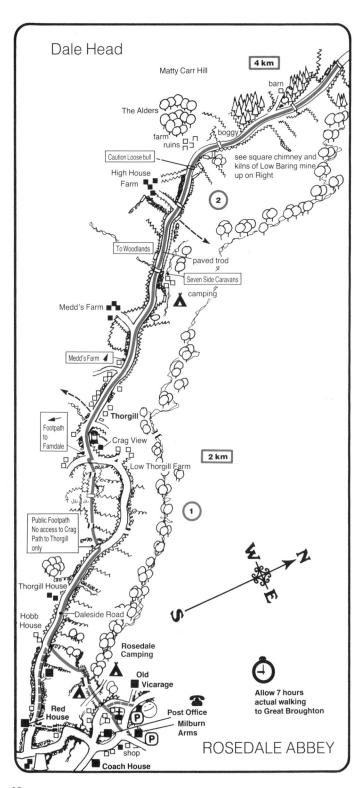

Dale Head

Matty Carr Hill

4 km

barn

The Alders

farm ruins

boggy

Caution Loose bull

see square chimney and kilns of Low Baring mine up on Right

High House Farm

2

To Woodlands

paved trod

Seven Side Caravans

camping

Medd's Farm

Medd's Farm

Thorgill

Footpath to Farndale

Crag View

2 km

Low Thorgill Farm

1

Public Footpath No access to Crag Path to Thorgill only

Thorgill House

Hobb House

Daleside Road

Rosedale Camping

Old Vicarage

☎ Post Office

Milburn Arms

Red House

shop

Coach House

ROSEDALE ABBEY

Allow 7 hours actual walking to Great Broughton

12

Lunch: From Rosedale Abbey, the excellent and recommended Lion Inn on Blakey Ridge is about two hours' walk, with five hours of easy walking to follow to Great Broughton. If the Lion appears to be too early on your schedule for lunch, or indeed if you are starting from the Lion, then a packed lunch will be necessary. (A pleasant picnic spot is indicated on page 16.)

Rosedale Abbey to Dale Head

Going: First a return along the dale lane by which we entered the village yesterday. After about an hour this becomes a pleasant grass track.

In the sixteenth century, glassworkers came to Rosedale from France to produce goblets, bottles and 'linen-smoothers'. The old kiln can now be seen in Ryedale Folk Museum (page 51), thanks to help from Pilkington's, the famous present-day glassmakers.

In 1860, before Rosedale's mining boom, the population of the valley was less than 600. Ten years later it had risen to nearly 3,000 and the valley was swarming with workers. The East Mines alone employed 100 men on each shift. It was said that some beds never got cold – as one man crawled out, another, from a different shift, climbed in. Now the population is down to below that of the pre-boom period. If you manage to visit the church of St Mary and St Lawrence notice a lintel from the old priory cloisters inscribed *Omnia Vanita* – All is vanity.

Leave Rosedale Abbey by yesterday's route through the campsite and along Daleside Road. Two or three minutes beyond Thorgill House take the signposted footpath on Left through gate and half-Right up field to join old walled walk. Rejoin road at Thorgill and continue along Daleside Road.

On a fine day this valley can become an idyllic pastoral retreat, away from the realities of the outside world. The tops of the protecting hills are covered in heather in September, and when the sun shines, soaring skylarks sing and unsuspecting grouse chortle. However, these same hills can hold the valley to siege, with dense mists, freezing blizzards and snow-drifts that can last from December to April. In February 1942 a wartime Spitfire crashed high up on Rosedale Bank on the left. The young fighter-pilot, with both legs broken, died alone there – not from his injuries, but from starvation.

During the iron-ore days 'drifts', or tunnels, were cut into the hillside above Medd's Farm. One of these ran for 1,500 feet *460 m* to the bottom of a vertical shaft. At the top of the shaft, hauling gear lifted the iron ore 270 feet *82 m* to the surface, where it was loaded directly onto wagons on the Rosedale railway. This mine, known as Sheriff's Pit, was worked from 1857 to 1911.

Near the caravan site on the Right can be seen further traces of a paved trod laid to ease the way of pack-horse trains on their way up the valley.

Just beyond High House Farm a notice on a gate across the bridleway warns of a loose bull! I have never met this fickle animal, which I am told is moved around the various fields here, but the Park Authority knows of its existence and suggests we should not be unduly worried. Fortunately, three gates later a further notice gives the 'all-clear'.

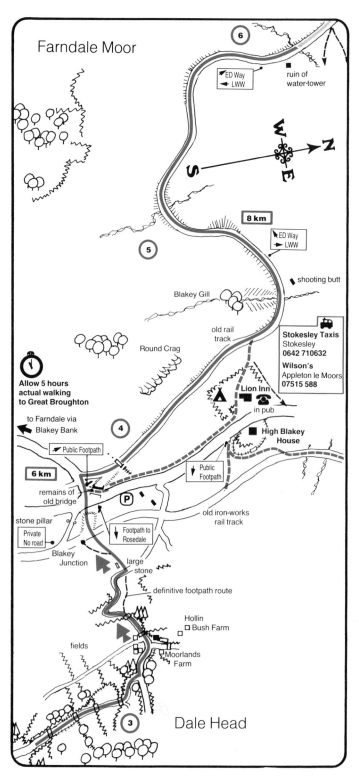

Dale Head to Farndale Moor

Going: A steep path leads up from the dale road to rejoin the iron-works railway track with its easy walking and marvellous views.

Through a series of gates to join a farm road, where turn Left into Moorlands Farm.

Raymond Hayes, in *A History of Rosedale,* relates how the pannier trod that we saw earlier once actually ran through the farmhouse here and consequently the doors were never locked! Eventually a new farmhouse was built, but the trod still ran through the garden.

Leave the farmyard by the road which climbs the dale side. Shortly after the second Right-hand bend, leave the road to take the waymarked track on the Left which climbs up through the bracken to the iron-works railway track.

This is the site of Blakey Junction, where loaded trains from the East Mines – where we were yesterday – joined the line running from Hollins Mines at Rosedale Bank Top and Sheriff's Pit. There was once a huddle of railway cottages here.

Cross the rail track to take the path running up the side of the cutting leading to the now filled-in bridge and the Castleton–Hutton road.

To visit the inn, turn Right for a ten-minute walk along the road verge. Leave the inn by paddock at rear, and pass through gap in far Right corner to join railway-track route.

The Lion Inn dates from 1553 and was a popular alehouse for the pack-horse 'jaggers' – the men in charge of the ponies. The 'jagger' name came about because the ponies were usually a type of sturdy hunting horse from Germany, now extinct, called jaggers, from the German word for hunter – Jäger. Gradually the name for a pack-horse train became a 'jag', and the man in charge, a 'jagger'. The inn was also an important marketplace for the sale of fish from the coast, and corn from the dales. An annual sheep fair still takes place here on the first Saturday in October.

If bypassing the inn, cross the road and take the road signposted down to Farndale. Immediately turn Right to walk along old railway-track footpath.

After two miles *3 km,* pass the ruins of a water-tower.

In 1916 a train was completely buried by snow and the crew and a lady passenger were obliged to spend a night in a hut here.

The line was never fenced, as travellers on the moors were few. Unfortunately however, sheep were prone to sleeping on the track, but it was cheaper to compensate the occasional irate farmer than pay for 20 miles *32 km* of fencing. Grouse can always be seen or heard along the line, and there are many stories of drivers who were wont to halt their engines to make welcome contributions to the pot.

We have now joined the Lyke Wake Walk, a route from Osmotherley (page 29) to Ravenscar, on the coast. The walk was pioneered by local farmer, Bill Cowley, in 1955, and the aim is to complete the gruelling 40 miles *64 km* in under 24 hours! The boots of over 80,000 participants have worn a wide scar across the moor in places. The name of the walk is taken from an ancient Cleveland dirge which suggests that the souls of the dead are obliged to take a walk across these moors.

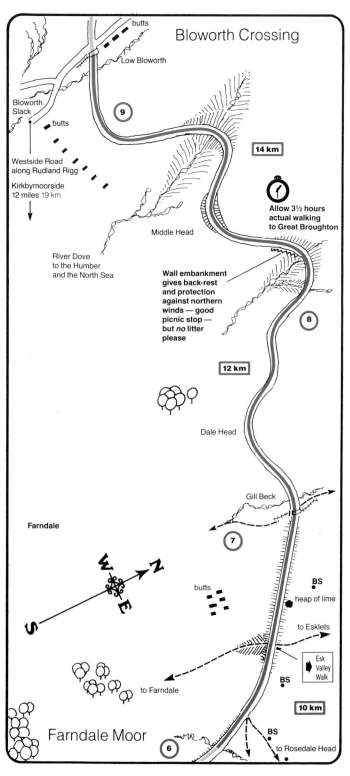

Bloworth Crossing

butts

Low Bloworth

(9)

Bloworth Slack

butts

Westside Road along Rudland Rigg

Kirkbymoorside 12 miles 19 km

Middle Head

River Dove to the Humber and the North Sea

14 km

Allow 3½ hours actual walking to Great Broughton

Wall embankment gives back-rest and protection against northern winds — good picnic stop — but *no* litter please

(8)

12 km

Dale Head

Gill Beck

(7)

Farndale

butts

BS

heap of lime

to Esklets

Esk Valley Walk

to Farndale

BS

10 km

Farndale Moor

(6)

BS

to Rosedale Head

16

Farndale Moor to Bloworth Crossing

Going: Savour these last three miles *5 km* of level walking which lead so easily across the centre of the moors.

Continue past footpath which goes off to Right to Esklets, and, after almost a mile *1.6 km* of straight embankment, through a gate at Gill Beck.

Esklets, once an ancient farmstead belonging to Rievaulx Abbey, is now in ruins. Here is the source of the River Esk, which flows into the North Sea at Whitby 30 miles *48 km* away. Winters have always presented problems here 1,300 feet *400 m* up on the moors, with high winds and heavy snow falls, and drifts on the line up to 20 feet *6 m* deep. During construction of the line here in January 1861, a sudden blizzard trapped 40 workmen, and they took shelter in temporary huts nearby. Conditions were so bad that the line's snowplough could not reach them. Work was held up for three weeks. Eventually a Mr King, a railway official, and the local constable bravely set off with shovels and food to try to find them. Although the huts were completely covered by snow, the men were eventually discovered. They were suffering from lack of food and fuel, but all were safely rescued.

It is claimed that sometimes snow can still be found here as late as June. I doubt if you will be looking for a snowplough on your Footpath Tour, but in case the weather is being a little unsporting, you may like to know that you can find a low wall between Dale Head and Middle Head – on the Left below the level of the track – which gives some kind of shelter from north-easters and provides a back-support and a very scenic picnic-stop; but please – no litter!

Farndale, down on the Left, is famous for its daffodils. No one is certain how the millions of small wild daffodils came to be there, but a local theory suggests the monks of Rievaulx Abbey may have originally been responsible. Once picked in their thousands, the daffodils became protected in 1953 by the establishment of a 2,000-acre nature reserve. When the flowers are in bloom the dale is crowded with visitors arriving by car and coach. In the late 1960s there were proposals to create a reservoir in this wild and beautiful valley. However the scheme was rejected by the House of Commons. Farndale may get its name from *fearna,* the Gaelic for alder.

Through the gate at Bloworth Crossing.

This was once a level-crossing for the busy pack-horse pannier-way, Westside Road, which runs along Rudland Rigg to Kirkbymoorside. There were crossing-keeper's cottages here, but these disappeared during battle-training in the 1939–45 war!

It is difficult to imagine the industry and noise which once disturbed the present stillness here, with the regular passage of labouring steam engines coaxing along clanking trains of up to fifteen loaded wagons at a time. Harry Mead, in his excellent *Inside the North York Moors,* estimates that 10 million tons of ore travelled along this line to the North-East iron and steel industry. The busiest year was 1873, when 560,668 tons were moved – over 1,500 tons per day.

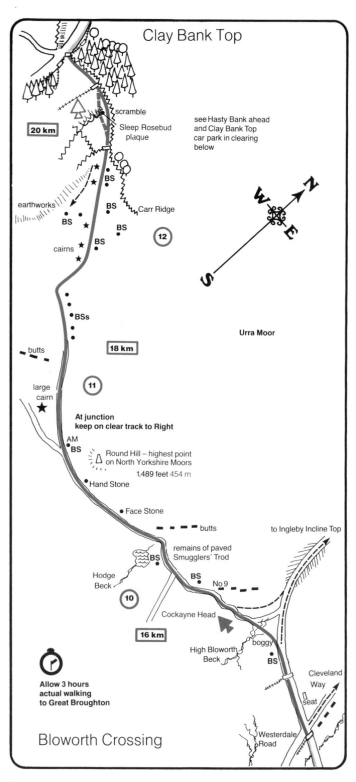

Clay Bank Top

scramble

Sleep Rosebud plaque

20 km

see Hasty Bank ahead
and Clay Bank Top
car park in clearing
below

BS
BS
Carr Ridge
earthworks
BS
BS
12
cairns
BS

Urra Moor

BSs

18 km

butts

large
cairn
11

At junction
keep on clear track to Right

AM
BS
Round Hill – highest point
on North Yorkshire Moors
1,489 feet 454 m

Hand Stone

Face Stone

butts

to Ingleby Incline Top

remains of paved
Smugglers' Trod

BS
BS
No 9

Hodge
Beck
10

Cockayne Head

16 km

boggy
BS

High Bloworth
Beck

Cleveland
Way

seat

Allow 3 hours
actual walking
to Great Broughton

Westerdale
Road

Bloworth Crossing

Bloworth Crossing to Clay Bank Top

Going: A clear wide track wanders up to Round Hill, the highest point on the North Yorkshire Moors, and continues, accompanied by cairns and ancient boundary stones, finally dropping down to the road at Clay Bank Top.

Just beyond a seat and a gate we leave the easy, level walking provided by nineteenth-century railway engineers, and bear Left on a wide track which begins with a little dampness at High Bloworth Beck and climbs to Cockayne Head.

On the Right it is possible to see sections of a paved way in places. This is known locally as the Smugglers' or Sailors' Trod, but it was in use as a trading route long before the smuggling of rum and tobacco became profitable. Unfortunately most of the paving slabs have now found their way into the construction of Cleveland farm buildings and grouse shooting butts.

The sticky yellow clay here was once widely used as a colour-wash in moorland cottages, while the reddish shale found in places served as 'reddle' for marking sheep.

Pass on the Left a track which runs down Cockayne Ridge, and the pond which marks the beginning of Hodge Beck.

Further along on the Right, notice a boundary stone with a Celtic-style carved face. This Face Stone is mentioned in a survey of the boundaries of Helmsley Estate conducted in 1642. A little further on is another boundary stone. Known as the Hand Stone, it has a rough carving of a hand on two sides. One bears the words: *This is the way to Stoxla,* and the other: *This is the way to Kirbie.* Stoxla is now Stokesley, seven miles *11 km* to the north-west, and Kirbie is Kirkbymoorside (page 47). This stone probably dates from 1711, when an order was made by justices at Northallerton for guideposts to be erected throughout the North Riding of Yorkshire.

White stone pillar on Right indicates highest point on moors.

The trig point is sited on an ancient stone barrow which is thought also to be the most northerly point of an ancient track, with the Danish name of *Thurkilstye,* which ran from York to Cleveland.

A large cairn marks a junction just beyond the trig point. Take the Right fork.

Track to Left – scarred out as a fire-break – goes to Bilsdale.

Continue on the wide Right-hand track, with its many cairns and boundary stones, as it rises slightly along Carr Ridge. Down at wall junction go through small gate.

Just before gate, off to the Left, can be seen prehistoric earthworks which run for three miles *4 km* along the escarpment. This ancient boundary is known locally as Cromwell's Trench.

Continue beyond gate with wall on Right. A scramble down through a crag can be avoided by keeping close to wall.

Those who choose to scramble may notice a very small brass plaque fixed to rocks on the Right in memory of a terrier which stole the show on a 1978 television programme marking the anniversary of the Lyke Wake Walk. *Sleep Rosebud of Kermansha, 1973–1981.*

With wall on Right, continue steeply down, through gate in fence, and through gate onto road at Clay Bank Top. Turn Right to proceed with care on this often busy road.

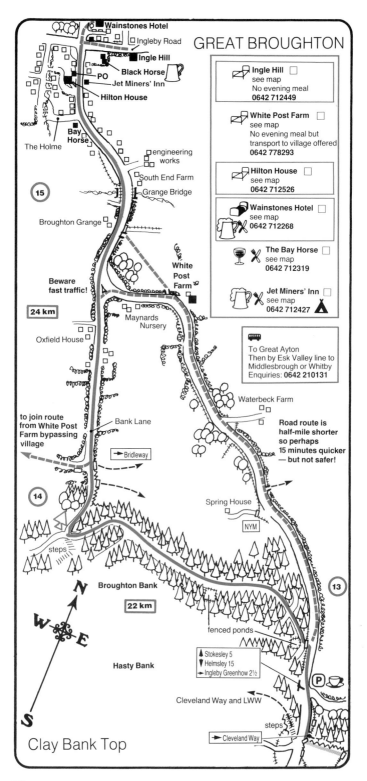

GREAT BROUGHTON

Wainstones Hotel
Ingleby Road
Ingle Hill
Black Horse
PO
Jet Miners' Inn
Hilton House
Bay Horse
The Holme

engineering works
South End Farm
Grange Bridge

(15)

Broughton Grange

White Post Farm

Beware fast traffic!

24 km

Maynards Nursery

Oxfield House

to join route from White Post Farm bypassing village

Bank Lane

→ Bridleway

(14)

steps

Broughton Bank

22 km

N
W E
S

Hasty Bank

Waterbeck Farm

Road route is half-mile shorter so perhaps 15 minutes quicker — but not safer!

Spring House

NYM

(13)

fenced ponds

▲ Stokesley 5
▼ Helmsley 15
→ Ingleby Greenhow 2½

Cleveland Way and LWW

steps

→ Cleveland Way

Clay Bank Top

Ingle Hill ☐
see map
No evening meal
0642 712449

White Post Farm ☐
see map
No evening meal but
transport to village offered
0642 778293

Hilton House ☐
see map
0642 712526

Wainstones Hotel ☐
see map
0642 712268

The Bay Horse ☐
see map
0642 712319

Jet Miners' Inn ☐
see map
0642 712427

To Great Ayton
Then by Esk Valley line to
Middlesbrough or Whitby
Enquiries: 0642 210131

20

Clay Bank Top to Great Broughton

Going: An easy end to a long day. Either take a forestry road along Broughton Bank, followed by a lane and road walk, or go all the way by road – marginally quicker, but beware of traffic!

Caution: If you are reading this guidebook aloud to a companion, keep this paragraph to yourself! The viewpoint of Clay Bank car park thoughtfully provides a refreshment hut. However, too many times have I swept into the clearing anticipating a mug of hot, life-giving tea – only to find it closed. So perhaps we should restrict the suspense to you and me alone. I hope you are lucky and find it open. If so rejoice, treat your companion – and have an extra cup for me!

During levelling work for this car park in 1969, the remains of a Bronze Age cemetery and crematorium were revealed. A flue and charred fragments of bone were identified.

Shortest route from here is down by road, shown on map (taking field path to cut off corner between White Post Farm and Broughton Grange). However the verges are not good, and the traffic travels too fast down the hill, so unless you can present a good reason, I recommend the forest route.

For this go through gate on Left a few yards down from the car park and turn Right onto forestry road. Follow this easy track over cross-road and past second fenced pond. Track drops down, and after passing a Left turn, the track bears to Left. At steps coming down on Left, take sharp Right turn down onto track which drops steeply to join Bank Lane.

If you are staying at White Post Farm, lane to Left offers short-cut, avoiding village, to Solomon's Porch (map, page 22).

At this point the route briefly leaves the National Park.

In 1952 some 550 square miles *1,425 sq. km* were designated as a national park, with boundaries largely drawn up by nature. On the east is the North Sea, and high cliffs which include Boulby Head, the highest on England's eastern coast. In the south are the Howardian Hills. The western and northern boundaries are formed by the spectacular escarpment of the Cleveland Hills. This perimeter runs for almost 150 miles *242 km*. Forty per cent of the park is open moorland, and twelve is taken up by the Forestry Commission. Park Authority headquarters are in the old Helmsley vicarage.

Continue ahead down Bank Lane. At Maynards Nursery join main road, with care, and continue into Great Broughton.

Great Broughton is a charming village which dates back 300 years, although Domesday Book makes reference to a *Broctun Magna*. About a mile *1.6 km* to east can be traced mounds which were once the medieval village of Little Broughton. Alum- and jet-mining have both been important in the village's history – note the Jet Miners' Inn. There was also once a busy cottage weaving industry.

Anyone staying at Hilton House (see the accommodation panel opposite) should note that it is the home of the writer and moors authority, Harry Mead. It takes only a few minutes of conversation for Harry's great enthusiasm for the moors to become apparent. He can knowledgeably answer any queries you may have. However, a word of warning! Make sure you catch him in the evening. Start him off in the morning and you will be hard pushed to get to Osmotherley by opening time!

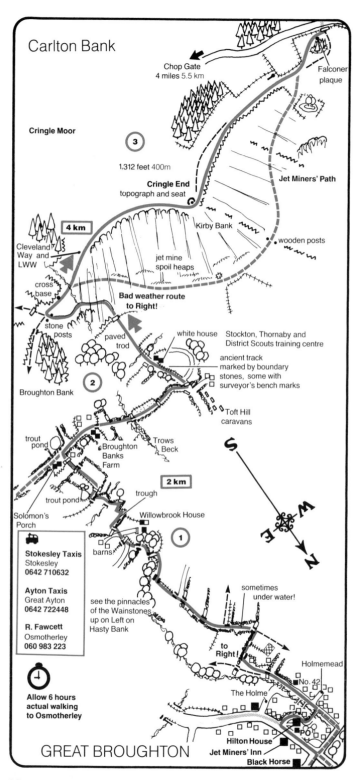

Carlton Bank

Cringle Moor

③

1,312 feet 400m

Chop Gate
4 miles 5.5 km

Falconer
plaque

Jet Miners' Path

Cringle End
topograph and seat

Kirby Bank

wooden posts

4 km

Cleveland
Way and
LWW

jet mine
spoil heaps

cross
base

**Bad weather route
to Right!**

stone
posts

white house

paved
trod

Stockton, Thornaby and
District Scouts training centre

ancient track
marked by boundary
stones, some with
surveyor's bench marks

Broughton Bank

②

Toft Hill
caravans

trout
pond

**Broughton
Banks
Farm**

Trows
Beck

2 km

trout pond

trough

Solomon's
Porch

Willowbrook House

①

barns

see the pinnacles
of the Wainstones
up on Left on
Hasty Bank

sometimes
under water!

**to
Right!**

Holmemead

Stokesley Taxis
Stokesley
0642 710632

Ayton Taxis
Great Ayton
0642 722448

R. Fawcett
Osmotherley
060 983 223

🕐
**Allow 6 hours
actual walking
to Osmotherley**

No. 42

The Holme

Hilton House
Jet Miners' Inn
Black Horse

GREAT BROUGHTON

Lunch: After about four hours of strenuous but rewarding walking you should reach the attractive village of Swainby, with its bridges, pubs, shops and toilets. (Mrs Stonehouse of the Miners' Arms – the first pub you get to – is renowned for her splendid homemade pies with mushy peas, but you need to phone 0642 700457 the night before, so she can soak the peas!) If you decline to visit Swainby, with its pleasures, and choose to take the Cleveland Way alternative, you save about a mile *1.6 km,* avoid some road walking – and you will need a packed lunch.

Great Broughton to Carlton Bank

Leave Great Broughton by Bakery Path near the post office and Hilton House. Cross footbridge over Bradley Beck and turn Left on road past ford and The Holme. Where houses end, and hedged lane turns up to Right, continue ahead over stile, with beck on Left. A footpath goes straight ahead, but bear Right, past horse-box, to cross stile in far Right corner of field. Continue with hedge on Left to cross second fence. Turn Left on track and over stile. Follow waymarks to pass Willowbrook House. Turn Right briefly at first trout pond, and emerge onto lane between buildings of Solomon's Porch.

If walking the White Post Farm alternative, rejoin here.

Turn Right on lane into Broughton Banks Farm and locate stile behind farmhouse. Cross field to gate and gap in hedge, and through gap to continue ahead with hedge on Left. Cross Trows Beck and, between hedges and fences, onto lane at Toft Hill, where turn Left onto ancient track. Steeply up track with white house (Scout training centre) on Right.

Worn paving-stones testify to the amount of traffic which once used this old pack-horse route to Kirkby and Stokesley.

Track climbs and bear Left to cross waterfall. At two stone posts turn Right, to walk with wall on Left.

We now rejoin the Cleveland Way and LWW route for the four miles *6 km* to Huthwaite Green. The stone base of the ancient Donna Cross bears the initials F–E and marks the boundary of the Feversham and Emmerson estates.

The route now ascends steeply to the rim of Kirby Bank and on to Cringle End.

The splendid viewpoint of Cringle End should not be missed. However if weather is unkind, and visibility poor, you may wish to avoid the climb of 315 feet 96 m by taking Jet Miners' Path, which goes off to Right immediately over the stream and continues below pink heaps of jet mine spoil and through old workings, staying on the same contour below Cringle End all the way round to rejoin the main route before the Carlton Bank road.

Jet is a fossilised wood found in shale beds, and it has been used for ornamental purposes since prehistoric times. In recent history it became immensely popular when Queen Victoria chose to wear it while mourning Prince Albert. Before beginning the ascent, diligent searchers prepared to poke about in the slurry to the Left may be rewarded by discovering a fragment.

From Cringle End, with its Falconer memorial seat and topograph, follow the worn tracks, with wall on the Right, down past fir-tree plantations on the Left, to the Carlton Bank road.

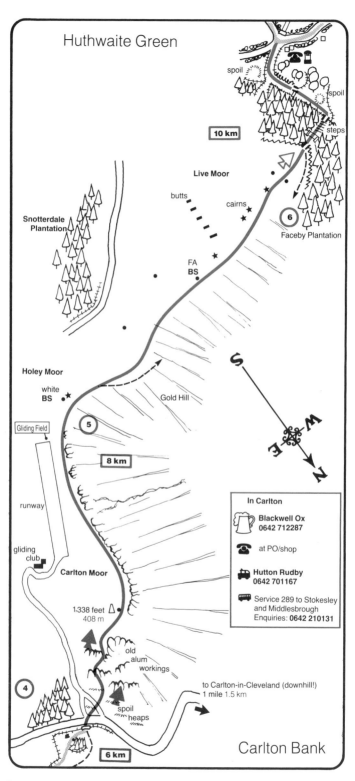

Huthwaite Green

spoil

spoil

steps

10 km

Live Moor

butts

cairns

Snotterdale
Plantation

⑥

Faceby Plantation

FA
BS

Holey Moor

white
BS

Gold Hill

Gliding Field

⑤

8 km

runway

gliding
club

Carlton Moor

1·338 feet △
408 m

In Carlton

Blackwell Ox
0642 712287

at PO/shop

Hutton Rudby
0642 701167

Service 289 to Stokesley
and Middlesbrough
Enquiries: 0642 210131

old
alum
workings

④

spoil
heaps

to Carlton-in-Cleveland (downhill!)
1 mile 1.5 km

6 km

Carlton Bank

Carlton Bank to Huthwaite Green

Going: A stiff climb of 354 feet *107 m* up onto Carlton Moor, followed by a scenic and easy descent to Huthwaite Green.

Cross Chop Gate–Carlton road and head for the remains of old alum mines on the mutilated heap of Carlton Moor ahead. Any of the multi-tracks ahead will do as long as they go up. On certain days you will need to be wary of motor-cycles, which leap like mechanised gazelles over the spoil heaps and appear in front of you with little warning!

Alum was in great demand from the fourteenth century for the leather-tanning and textile-dyeing industries, and at the end of the fifteenth century Britain's first mine was established on the moors. Previously alum was only available from mines owned by the Vatican. The method of production of alum from the mined shale was lengthy and bizarre. It involved calcining the shale (reducing it to a powder by heat), mixing with water and boiling for 24 hours. The result was then mixed with burned seaweed – kelp – and human urine. Enormous amounts of seaweed were required – 20 tons only making one ton of kelp. The urine was shipped in large quantities from London by pack-horse trains. There were also local purchases, with the going price being one penny per gallon. The foul mixture then underwent various settling and crystallisation stages before it was packed in barrels and sold. About 130 tons of shale were required to produce a ton of alum. At one time there were over 20 quarries in the area. However, the high costs of production and the introduction of new sources eventually brought about the decline of the industry in the area and the last mine closed in 1871. This particular mine on Carlton Bank was the largest of the inland mines, and was worked from 1680 to 1809. Its annual production was about 250 tons, which was about half that of larger mines on the coast.

The bike-riders are from the York Youth Motor-cycle Club, and technically all are 'authorised riders'.

From the trig point and boundary stone at the top, keep to the Right along the rim of the escarpment to stay clear of the gliding club runway. The route is well walked and is accompanied by various boundary stones standing out from the heather.

The views over the Cleveland Plain are spectacular. On a clear day the line of the Pennines can be seen 40 miles *64 km* to the west. To the north are Middlesbrough and industrial Teeside. Roseberry Topping, which was seen from Danby Rigg on the first day of the tour, is now visible from another angle, as is the pillar of Captain Cook's memorial on Easby Moor. Nearer is the 777-foot *237 m* tree-covered Whorl Hill.

There is a slight rise to the summit of Live Moor at 1,025 feet *312 m,* and then the path drops down to the trees of Faceby Plantation and a steeply stepped sheep drift. Emerging down below trees, turn Left to follow the clear path round to the road at Huthwaite (or Heathwaite) Green.

Beyond the trees on the Left of the path are all that remain of the workings of the Marquis of Aislesbury's Scugdale Iron Mine, which in 1880 produced 66,000 tons of ore. A tramway serving the line once ran through the gate opposite the telephone box.

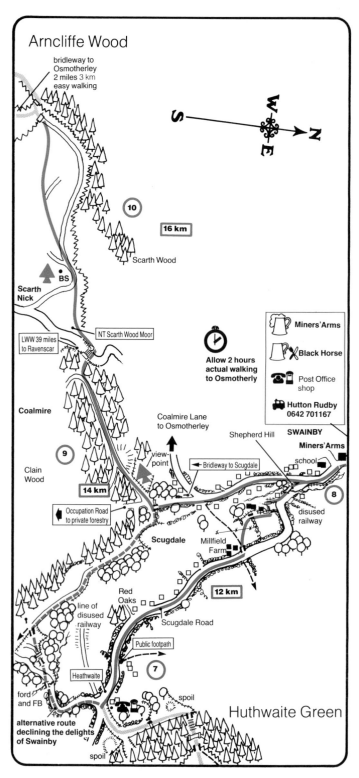

Arncliffe Wood

bridleway to
Osmotherley
2 miles 3 km
easy walking

⑩

16 km

Scarth Wood

Scarth
Nick

BS

NT Scarth Wood Moor

LWW 39 miles
to Ravenscar

Allow 2 hours
actual walking
to Osmotherly

Coalmire

Coalmire Lane
to Osmotherley

Shepherd Hill

⑨

view-
point

Bridleway to Scugdale

SWAINBY

Miners' Arms

school

Clain
Wood

14 km

Occupation Road
to private forestry

Scugdale

Millfield
Farm

disused
railway

⑧

Red
Oaks

line of
disused
railway

Scugdale Road

12 km

Public footpath

⑦

Heathwaite

spoil

ford
and FB

Huthwaite Green

alternative route
declining the delights
of Swainby

spoil

Legend box:

🍺 Miners' Arms

🍺✗ Black Horse

☎ Post Office
shop

🚍 Hutton Rudby
0642 701167

26

Huthwaite Green to Arncliffe Wood

Going: Easy lane walking provides a pleasant detour down into the village of Swainby for a lunch-stop. Back up onto a forest track on Coalmire, followed by a fine moorland stretch to Arncliffe Wood. A mile is saved by taking the Cleveland Way route avoiding the village.

At road turn right for easy walk of just over one mile *1.6 km* **down lane to the village of Swainby.**

If you intend to continue on Cleveland Way route to bypass Swainby, cross the road and take farm lane down to ford and footbridge. Tractor track forks Right to second ford and footbridge in trees. Through gate into field. Farm track veers Left but head for far Right corner to cross stile onto very pleasant forestry track. Turn Right to rejoin main route at sharp Left bend.

There is some confusion about whether this tiny hamlet in Scugdale is Heathwaite or Huthwaite. OS maps identify it as Huthwaite, however the road sign clearly names it Heathwaite. In 1890 the world's tallest living man, at 8ft 6in. *2.59 m,* left this tiny dale to join the famous circus of Barnum and Bailey. His name was familiar – Henry Cooper!

Immediately beyond Millfield Farm, take footpath on Left to far Right corner of field to pass behind buildings of Mill Farm then Left onto farm drive and Right to rejoin road. Turn Left to cross footbridge at ford, and turn Right on Coalmire Lane into village.

Immediately before the ford, a gate and hedges on the Right mark the line of the Scugdale Iron Mines tramway mentioned earlier. It was these mines which made Swainby into a mining village. The first pub you come to is the Miners' Arms – mention *Footpath-Touring* for a friendly welcome. There are two other pubs – both offering food – further down the attractive wide village street, with its central beck and bridges. The Church of The Holy Cross was built in the 1870s, and contains a wooden cross specially carved for the church by a leading wood-carver in Oberammergau.

Leave Swainby by returning along Coalmire Lane, but continue ahead where Shepherd Hill lane bears Left. Further on, where lane bears Right, take hedged track ahead, signposted to Scugdale. At top of lane, go through gate and turn Right onto forestry road which rises steeply – and initially muddily – in Clain Wood. Cleveland Way and non-Swainby detour rejoin at this gate.

At junction of tracks note spoil tip, a fine viewpoint.

Where main forestry track bears Left, take path ahead through trees, which drops onto the road at Scarth Nick.

This cleft, gouged out by the melt-waters of an Ice Age, was used by the old cattle-drovers on their long journey from Scotland to the south. They forded the River Tees at Yarm, crossed the Cleveland Plain, passed through Swainby and herded their charges through this gap to climb up onto the western rim of the moors. We rejoin this drovers' route tomorrow on Hambleton, after Osmotherley.

Turn Left over cattle-grid and immediately turn Right to go up on Scarth Wood Moor with wall on Right. Continue on well-walked track through heather, until wall on Right sweeps round to rejoin route at junction of walls and stile and gate.

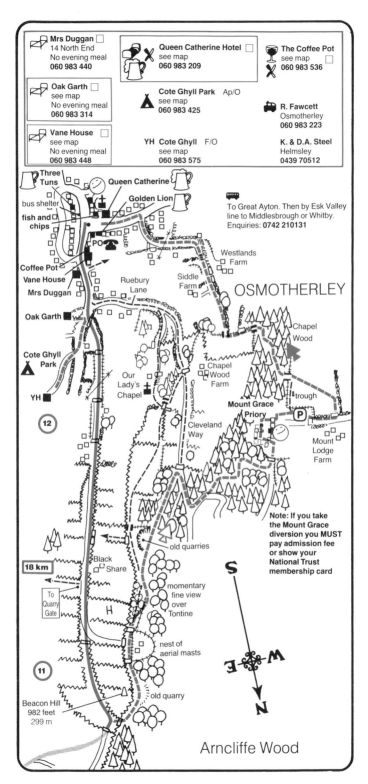

Mrs Duggan
14 North End
No evening meal
060 983 440

Oak Garth
see map
No evening meal
060 983 314

Vane House
see map
No evening meal
060 983 448

Queen Catherine Hotel
see map
060 983 209

Cote Ghyll Park Ap/O
see map
060 983 425

YH Cote Ghyll F/O
see map
060 983 575

The Coffee Pot
see map
060 983 536

R. Fawcett
Osmotherley
060 983 223

K. & D.A. Steel
Helmsley
0439 70512

Three Tuns

bus shelter

Queen Catherine

Golden Lion

fish and chips

PO

Coffee Pot

Vane House

Mrs Duggan

Oak Garth

Cote Ghyll Park

YH

(12)

Ruebury Lane

Siddle Farm

Westlands Farm

OSMOTHERLEY

To Great Ayton. Then by Esk Valley line to Middlesbrough or Whitby. Enquiries: 0742 210131

Chapel Wood

Our Lady's Chapel

Chapel Wood Farm

Cleveland Way

Mount Grace Priory

trough

P

Mount Lodge Farm

18 km

To Quarry Gate

Black Share

H

old quarries

momentary fine view over Tontine

nest of aerial masts

old quarry

Note: If you take the Mount Grace diversion you MUST pay admission fee or show your National Trust membership card

S

E W

N

(11)

Beacon Hill
982 feet
299 m

Arncliffe Wood

28

Arncliffe Wood to Osmotherley

Going: A level, walled bridleway will have you in Osmotherley in just over half an hour. However a fairly rugged diversion of about three miles *5 km* will enable you to visit the beautifully kept remains of the fourteenth-century Mount Grace Priory.
Important: There is no right-of-way through the priory grounds, so if you take this route you MUST pay the admission fee (or show your National Trust membership card)!

At junction of walls, cross stile and bear Left to walk with wall on Right. This old track will conduct you directly and unerringly into hospitable Osmotherley.

For Mount Grace Priory, at junction of walls, cross stile and continue on the Cleveland Way LWW route by going through the gate on the Right to walk with wall on Left.

Continue behind fenced-off nest of assorted communications aerials. At this point it is often sensible to divert a little to the Right to avoid the mud churned up by thousands of boots beneath the trees, and also to get a glimpse of the fine view over the Vale of Mowbray with the Pennine Hills beyond.

At old quarry on Left a track close by wall leads over fields to Our Lady's Chapel. Note that path is certainly NOT a right-of-way, but it is walked. The chapel had a licence granted in 1397 for Mass to be said, and Carthusian monks probably lived here while they built their monastery below. The chapel was rebuilt in 1960, and during 1967 was visited by over ten thousand pilgrims.

Mount Grace Priory path now drops steeply down to arrive at a gate onto a field track. Do not follow the Cleveland Way through the gate but turn very sharp Right to take the lower of two forestry roads. Take the Left turn, and in a few yards leave the road for a wide grass track, Left, which twists down towards the priory. Note that this track is not a right-of-way, but I have received permission to include it in the Footpath Tour from the Forestry Commission and Arncliffe and Rounton Estates. *(There is a request that dogs be kept on a lead to protect young pheasants.)* At the usually locked priory gate on Left, . climb over – there is no stile – and into priory grounds, but do remember that you are required to find the office to pay for admission or present your National Trust card. Please observe this. *Open mid-March to mid-October: Monday to Saturday from 9.30 to 18.30 hrs, Sunday from 14.00 to 18.30 hrs; mid-October to mid-March: Monday to Saturday from 9.30 to 16.00 hrs, Sunday from 14.00 to 16.00 hrs. Informative guidebook on sale.*

The priory, founded in 1398, belonged to the Carthusian order, and is the best preserved in Britain. The monks lived as virtual hermits in individual cells, one of which has been carefully restored. Note the right-angled food hatch to prevent any contact between server and inmate. Remains include the priory church and cloisters.

There is a well-walked path from car park along field, with Chapel Wood on Left to footbridge/stile. *Correct right-of-way route is as shown on map opposite.* Over footbridge/stile, take path which climbs steeply up through trees. At decrepit stile enter field and after few yards, cross stile on Right onto field footpath which becomes Siddle Farm track into Osmotherley.

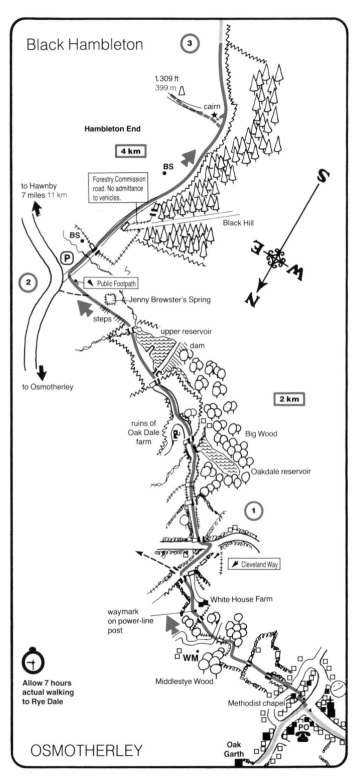

Black Hambleton

③

1,309 ft
399 m △
cairn

Hambleton End

4 km

BS

Forestry Commission
road. No admittance
to vehicles.

Black Hill

to Hawnby
7 miles 11 km

BS

P

②

← Public Footpath

Jenny Brewster's Spring

steps

to Osmotherley

upper reservoir

dam

2 km

ruins of
Oak Dale
farm

Big Wood

Oakdale reservoir

①

↖ Cleveland Way

White House Farm

waymark
on power-line
post

WM

Middlestye Wood

Methodist chapel

Allow 7 hours
actual walking
to Rye Dale

PO

Oak
Garth

OSMOTHERLEY

Lunch: The village of Hawnby is about four hours' walk, so an early start should get you to the pleasant Hawnby Hotel for lunch.

Osmotherley to Black Hambleton

Going: An interesting walk takes you easily up to the fine moorland Hambleton Drove Road.

Osmotherley was once a busy market-town on the edge of the moors. Today it presents a charming combination of old stone cottages and superbly sited modern homes. If you enter by the priory route, note 1757 Hermitage on the Left. Osmotherley is in no great hurry; Thompson's shop was established in 1788. Exactly two hundred years later – in 1988 – we noticed they had a calendar on display for 1979! On the square is the old Butter Cross; the stone slab nearby was probably used to display garden produce for sale, and evangelist John Wesley is said to have preached from it. Be certain to find time to visit the public toilets by the village hall. They are imaginatively cared for by Ann Cation – remember to thank her if you see her! The Queen Catherine is 'official' headquarters of Lyke Wake walkers and a copy of the fearful Cleveland Dirge is displayed in the bar. It is estimated that as many as 1,000 hopefuls accept the Lyke Wake challenge on some summer weekends. The present record for covering the 42 rugged miles *68 km* to Ravenscar is said to be five hours.

Leave Osmotherley by the 'ginnel' or narrow passage, behind the war memorial, signposted to the Methodist chapel.

Bearing the date 1754 above the door, this is thought to be one of the oldest Methodist chapels in the country.

Cross a back lane onto a hedged track, cross a field and down steps in trees to cross a stream. Over farm track and continue ahead to the waymarked electricity pole at White House Farm. Through stile by drive entrance onto lane, where turn Right. At main road, turn Left for few yards and turn Right through gate onto wide grass track. Through two fields, track drops down to stone bridge and Oakdale reservoir. Continue on obvious path to walk along by second reservoir.

The reservoirs, built in 1891 and 1910, supply Northallerton.

Cross footbridge and follow path up, stepped in places, past fenced Jenny Brewster's Spring, and through the bracken to the car park at sharp bend in Osmotherley–Hawnby road.

Turn Right on drovers' road, to walk with Black Hill plantation on Right.

We are back on the drovers' road that we crossed at Scarth Nick yesterday. Your legs may prompt the question of why the drovers chose to drive their charges up onto this high-level route instead of keeping to the gentler Vale of Mowbray. The answer is that up here on the Hambleton Road there were no toll charges. Cattle- and sheep-droving were once big business. Before refrigeration, the only methods of preserving meat were by smoking or salting. Normally it was necessary to consume meat soon after slaughter. This meant moving the meat as near as possible to the point of consumption while it was still alive! Huge droves were driven incredible distances to meet the demands of the big cities.

For diversion to high point of Black Hambleton, tractor tracks by cairn on Left lead to trig point.

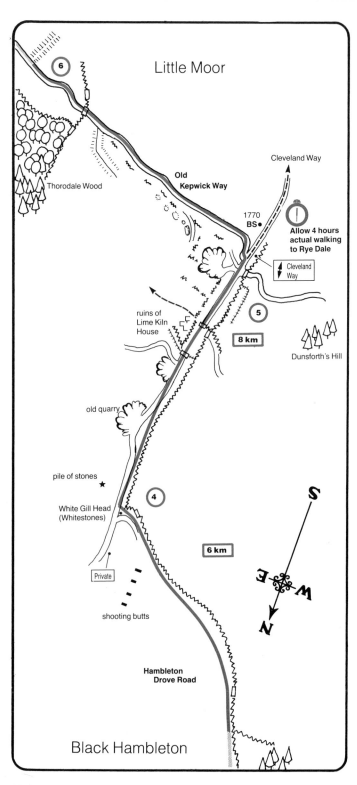

Little Moor

6

Thorodale Wood

Old
Kepwick Way

Cleveland Way

1770
BS●

Allow 4 hours
actual walking
to Rye Dale

Cleveland
Way

ruins of
Lime Kiln
House

5

8 km

Dunsforth's Hill

old quarry

pile of stones

4

6 km

White Gill Head
(Whitestones)

Private

shooting butts

Hambleton
Drove Road

Black Hambleton

Black Hambleton to Little Moor

Going: The limestone beneath the ancient drovers' road quickly drains away surface water to provide wonderful, mud-free, moorland walking.

This route was known to both Bronze Age man and the Romans. It is believed that Edward II and his army fled along this road in 1332, hotly pursued by Robert the Bruce. Seven miles *11 km* south of here, at a place still called Scotch Corner, the chase ended, and Edward was defeated. Three years later he was deposed and most cruelly murdered.

At White Gill Head junction, turn Right to continue with wall still on Right. Pass, on Left, old quarry and ruins of Lime Kiln House.

This was once a busy drovers' inn, providing overnight accommodation and sustenance for both drover and cattle. It was normal for a drover to handle a herd of up to 200 head of cattle, working with two dogs for every 50 beasts. On reaching market, the job of the drover was over and he began his journey back to pick up another commission. There is a legend that some drovers were in the habit of sending their dogs home ahead of them to save on the cost of their upkeep. The dogs could travel faster than the drover, knew the route, and also knew inns and farms which would supply them with food. The drover would pay the bill when he followed a few days later. Drovers were a colourful breed, and the job, although hard, had many attractions. In the sixteenth century it became necessary to pass an act restricting droving to licence-holders in an effort to discourage those seeking 'to leave their honest labour, and only to live easily'. A requirement was that all applicants should be married householders of at least 30 years of age.

Lime Kiln House last had a beer-selling licence in 1879. Although there is no sign of the kiln that gave the pub its name, there must have been one nearby, and its trade no doubt provided more customers. Limestone kilns were once kept very busy in this area producing lime for use as a building mortar, and especially for farmers to spread on their land to sweeten acid soil. These kilns often consisted of a round tower with an open domed fireplace. Limestone was tipped into a pit in the top of the tower where it was calcined – reduced to a powder – by the heat. Limestone is still quarried in the Vale of Pickering, but lime burning on the moors died out between 1870 and 1880. Harry Mead, in *Inside the Yorkshire Moors*, relates how farmers would journey to the lime kilns, taking with them coal dug from small local pits. The coal fuelled the kilns, and was accepted as part payment for the treated lime.

At cross-roads take a last look over the wall at the Vale of Mowbray in the direction of the Yorkshire dales of Swaledale and Wensleydale, and turn Left onto the Old Kepwick Way. Soft grass is now replaced by a road of stone chippings.

We leave the line of the Cleveland Way here until rejoining it for the last time between Rievaulx and Helmsley. This 93-mile *150 km* long-distance path was established in 1969 by the Countryside Commission, and runs from Helmsley to Filey near Scarborough, largely following the perimeter of the National Park.

Continue along Kepwick road, with signs of local quarrying on the Left, towards the corner of Thorodale Wood.

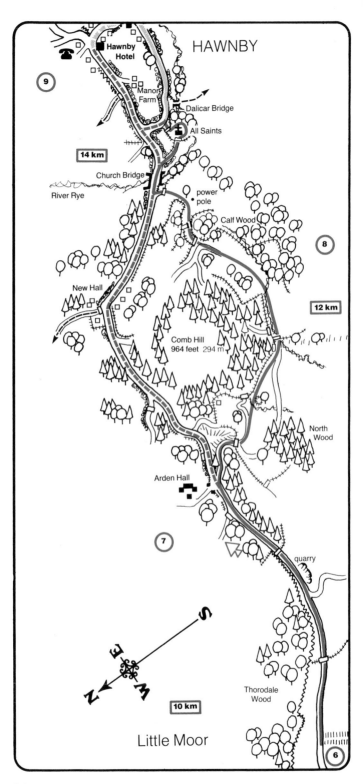

HAWNBY

Hawnby Hotel

Manor Farm

Dalicar Bridge

All Saints

14 km

Church Bridge

River Rye

power pole

Calf Wood

New Hall

Comb Hill
964 feet 294 m

12 km

North Wood

Arden Hall

quarry

Thorodale Wood

Little Moor

10 km

34

Little Moor to Hawnby

Going: Down into Hawnby with a choice of routes. Quickest is to stay on this quiet road. The recommended route skirts the distinctive, fir-tree-covered Comb Hill.

In his guide to the Cleveland Way, Bill Cowley tells how on Sunny Bank, a mile *1.6 km* to the south, an excavated tumulus revealed that about AD 700 a young Anglian girl of high rank was buried with her rich collection of bronze, gold and silver ornaments, and blue glass jewellery.

With the wall of Thorodale Wood on the Left, continue ahead on road, passing a farm track and quarry on the Right.

Over the wall on the Left can be glimpsed a small lake. This is in the grounds of Arden Hall, once the site of the small twelfth-century Benedictine nunnery of St Andrew which was dissolved under Henry VIII's 1536 Act for the Suppression of Lesser Monasteries. The land came into the possession of the Tancred family in 1574, and the local story is that Mary Queen of Scots spent a night here a few years before her execution. The present seventeenth-century Arden Hall is now the seat of the Earls of Mexborough.

Almost opposite the gates of Arden Hall, take a track which rises to Right through firs, and through gate into meadow. This section is not a right-of-way, but permission from Arden Estates allows it to be included in our Footpath Tour.

Those in a hurry to get to Hawnby Hotel for shelter or refreshment could stay on the road and be there in half an hour!

In meadow follow track which skirts round the base of fir-covered Comb Hill and rises to Calf Wood. Where this track turns sharply Left uphill, go through gate onto fenced track. Through gate into field and drop down past waymarked power pole to the fine Church Bridge over the Rye. Turn Right on road.

Church Bridge was designed by John Carr, whose work includes the building in York that houses the Castle Museum, and the famous Crescent in Buxton, Derbyshire.

I hope time allows you to make the short detour down Church Walk, on the Right, to visit the little church of All Saints.

There has been a church here beside the River Rye since the twelfth century. In the spring the churchyard is a mass of miniature daffodils. The village is proud of the way its men responded in the great wars. Two pages of the *Yorkshire Herald* of 23 October 1916 are displayed, acknowledging the patriotism of the parish and recording that, in the third year of the war, 46 men had already volunteered to serve. The war memorial shows that seventeen failed to return. The stained-glass west window, with its unusual design showing a wounded man and army stretcher-bearers, remembers 'those from this parish', and four German airmen of 7 Squadron of the *Luftwaffe* who were 'killed in action over Hawnby, 17 December, 1942'. I wonder if the families in Germany know that their men are remembered in this little church.

If you are heading for Hawnby Hotel then continue ahead. If you have no desire to go into 'up-town' Hawnby – as it is known – then you may take lane from church past Dalicar Bridge and the post office/shop to rejoin the route in 'down-town' Hawnby.

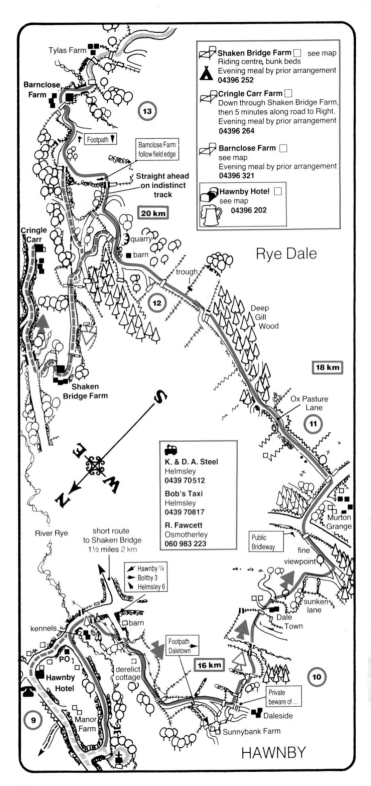

Tylas Farm

Barnclose Farm

⑬

↑ Footpath ↓

Barnclose Farm
follow field edge

Straight ahead
on indistinct
track

20 km

Cringle Carr

quarry

barn

trough

Rye Dale

⑫

Deep
Gill
Wood

Shaken
Bridge Farm

18 km

Ox Pasture
Lane

⑪

Murton
Grange

S

E

W

N

K. & D. A. Steel
Helmsley
0439 70512

Bob's Taxi
Helmsley
0439 70817

R. Fawcett
Osmotherley
060 983 223

Public
Bridleway

fine
viewpoint

River Rye

short route
to Shaken Bridge
1½ miles 2 km

⬈ Hawnby ¼
▶ Boltby 3
◀ Helmsley 6

sunken
lane

kennels

barn

Dale
Town

PO

Hawnby
Hotel

derelict
cottage

Footpath
Daletown

16 km

⑩

⑨

Manor
Farm

Private
beware of ...

Daleside

Sunnybank Farm

HAWNBY

Shaken Bridge Farm ☐ see map
Riding centre, bunk beds
Evening meal by prior arrangement
04396 252

Cringle Carr Farm ☐
Down through Shaken Bridge Farm,
then 5 minutes along road to Right.
Evening meal by prior arrangement
04396 264

Barnclose Farm ☐
see map
Evening meal by prior arrangement
04396 321

Hawnby Hotel! ☐
see map
04396 202

36

Hawnby to Rye Dale

Going: A delightful farm track and field walk to a splendid viewpoint. A farm lane and often muddy woodland path leading to the west bank of beautiful Rye Dale.

Leave 'up-town' Hawnby down Helmsley road to cross bridge over the River Rye. Immediately past the boarding kennels on the Right, cross stile into field and walk with hedge on Right.

In the kennel grounds can be seen a pond with fine collection of freshwater birds and some magnificent black swans.

In few yards bear Left down to far Left corner of field, and over stile into lane. Turn Right to cross cattle-grid and up open lane. Where Right fork goes up to Sunnybank Farm, keep Left on open lane. Through white gate and turn Left down signposted bridleway before cattle-grid entrance to Daleside.

Through next white gate, with fence on Right, and in few yards through gate on Right, then turn Left to go through small gate ahead. Walk down field to cross stile and footbridge in bottom of Gowerdale. Continue ahead steeply up to join farm track into Dale Town Farm. Through farmyard and, where road turns Left, bear Right by tree to walk up alongside sunken, and usually flooded, track and fence on Right. Where hedge on Right ends, turn Right to follow track heading for forest. Take thin track which curves up Left to join wide grass track from forest, which runs up hillside to road.

If a fine day, pause to reflect on the view across little-known Gowerdale to Hawnby. Behind the village, the masses of Hawnby Hill and Easterside lie like two sleeping giants, silent witnesses to the slow unfolding of man's history.

Cross road, and just beyond Murton Grange, turn Left onto Ox Pasture Lane and continue, to enter Deep Gill Wood. Keep to boundary wall on Left. As this sunless track is often muddy, it's best to beat a path through undergrowth along by wall.

On leaving wood, continue ahead through field, with fence on Left. Join track which runs down with barn on Right. Track divides at gate.

For Shaken Bridge Farm or Cringle Carr, take Left-hand grass track down to dale bottom.

Continue on track down to Right. Where this turns round to Left in few yards at cattle-grid, bear Right to follow indistinct track, with fence and bushes on Left, and cross stile ahead into field. Turn Left to follow hedge and fence to join track from Hagg Wood. Stay on this track, which drops down to Barnclose Farm. Bear Right through farm and down on road to cross stream and climb to go through Tylas Farm.

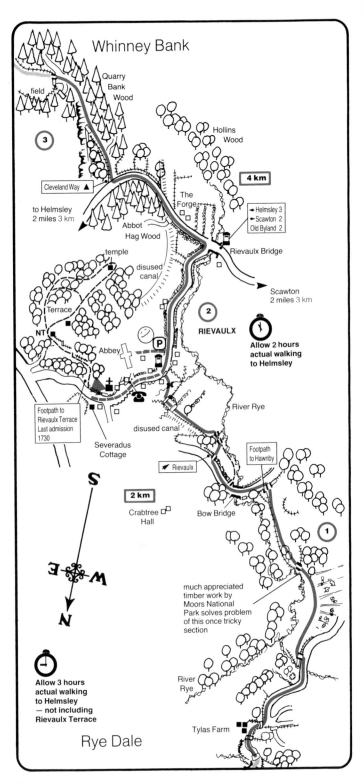

Whinney Bank

Quarry Bank Wood

field

Hollins Wood

Cleveland Way ▲

4 km

The Forge

→ Helmsley 3
← Scawton 2
Old Byland 2

to Helmsley
2 miles 3 km

Abbot Hag Wood

Rievaulx Bridge

temple

disused canal

→ Scawton
2 miles 3 km

Terrace

2

NT

RIEVAULX

Abbey

P

Allow 2 hours
actual walking
to Helmsley

Footpath to
Rievaulx Terrace
Last admission
1730

River Rye

Severadus
Cottage

disused canal

✈ Rievaulx

Footpath
to Hawnby

2 km

Crabtree
Hall

Bow Bridge

1

S

much appreciated
timber work by
Moors National
Park solves problem
of this once tricky
section

N
E · W

Allow 3 hours
actual walking
to Helmsley
— not including
Rievaulx Terrace

River
Rye

Tylas Farm

Rye Dale

Lunch: Helmsley offers excellent eating facilities.

Rye Dale to Whinney Bank

Going: A pleasant river-meadow walk into Rievaulx, with its fine abbey ruins and scenic terrace above. A short road walk out of village leads to a steep climb up to Whinney Bank.

Leave Tylas Farm by gate and follow road which bears down Left. At bottom of hill and stream, cross stile on Left into field and along bottom of shrub-covered slope until joining the tree-lined River Rye. Continue across often boggy meadow with fence on Left. At road, turn Left to cross Bow Bridge.

This is another example of the work of bridge-builder John Carr.

Note stile on Right immediately beyond Bow Bridge. **Official route is a few yards further on, by trees on Right, where cross over signposted stile into field, and half Left over double stile by river. Turn Left to follow fenced disused canal.**

It is believed that this canal, a quarter-mile *400 m* long, was built by the monks of Rievaulx in the twelfth century to transport stone from local quarries for use in the building of their great abbey. A stone weir was recently discovered where the canal left the river by the double stile.

Through gates and by barn onto road in village of Rievaulx – pronounced 'Reevo'. Tour route lies to Right, past the abbey, but interesting detour to Left leads to Rievaulx Terrace.

Just beyond church of St Mary the Virgin, the Terrace path is signposted on Right and zigzags very steeply up through trees to NT admission-ticket office and shop.

Landscaped in 1758, a half-mile-long 800 m lawn is curved to give superb and varied views over the abbey ruins. At one end is a Grecian-style Ionic temple, richly furnished and with a magnificent ceiling which took artist Guiseppe Borgnis eight years to paint. At the far end of the terrace is a Doric rotunda. Open daily, 1 April to end October: 10.30 to 17.30 hrs.

The abbey, once one of the largest and most splendid Cistercian abbeys in England, was founded in 1131. By the end of the century practically all the monastic buildings were complete, with an establishment of 140 monks and 500 lay brothers. Cistercians were very successful farmers, particularly with sheep, of which at one time they owned more than 14,000. They were also involved in milling, beekeeping, fishing, charcoal production and operating an iron furnace. However, by the end of the thirteenth century the abbey was heavily in debt, and decline followed. There were only 22 monks left by the time of Henry's Dissolution. Lead was taken from the roof, and the buildings soon collapsed. (The lead was melted into ingots and, strangely, buried and forgotten. It was rediscovered 400 years later and used in the restoration of the Five Sisters Window in York Minster.) The ruins today indicate the original beauty of the high walls, great Gothic arches and windows, and two fine cloisters. *Open every day. Admission fee. Exhibition.*

Continue on road to Rievaulx Bridge and turn Left on road, passing remains of a second abbey canal. At Cleveland Way sign, turn Right, steeply up through Quarry Bank Wood, along base of quarry cliffs on Left. At top of Whinney Bank, go through gate into field.

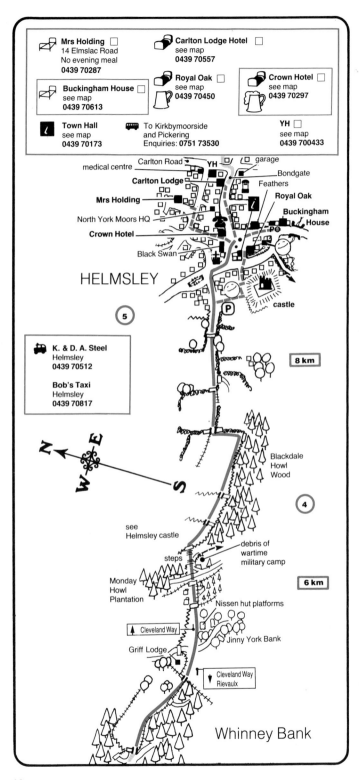

Mrs Holding ☐
14 Elmslac Road
No evening meal
0439 70287

Buckingham House ☐
see map
0439 70613

Carlton Lodge Hotel ☐
see map
0439 70557

Royal Oak ☐
see map
0439 70450

Crown Hotel ☐
see map
0439 70297

Town Hall
see map
0439 70173

To Kirkbymoorside
and Pickering
Enquiries: **0751 73530**

YH ☐
see map
0439 700433

medical centre — Carlton Road — **YH** — garage
Carlton Lodge — Bondgate — Feathers
Mrs Holding — **Royal Oak**
Buckingham House
North York Moors HQ
Crown Hotel
Black Swan

HELMSLEY

⑤

castle

K. & D. A. Steel
Helmsley
0439 70512

Bob's Taxi
Helmsley
0439 70817

P

8 km

Blackdale
Howl
Wood

④

see
Helmsley castle

steps

debris of
wartime
military camp

6 km

Monday
Howl
Plantation

Nissen hut platforms

↑ Cleveland Way

Jinny York Bank

Griff Lodge

↓ Cleveland Way
Rievaulx

Whinney Bank

Whinney Bank to Helmsley

Going: Easy field walking into Helmsley.

Along field with Whinney Bank Wood on Right. Cross track near ornate Griff Lodge. Continue with wall on Left.

From the terrace of Jinny York Bank there are splendid views to the Right. 240 feet *73 m* below in the valley runs the River Rye. Beyond are the woods on Castle Hill and Helmsley Windypit. In trees on the Right of the path can be traced concrete platforms which mark the site of a military camp which housed various units during the Second World War. (See memorial panels in Helmsley church.)

There are steps in a little up-and-down at Monday Howl, then through gate onto field path to walk with boundary of Blackdale Howl Wood on Right. Continue through gates to a sharp Left-and-Right turn, adjusting the line of the path, which becomes little lane into Helmsley. A footpath through the coach and car park on the Right (toilets) leads to Helmsley castle.

Impressive, grass-covered earthworks surround the castle site and tall Norman keep, with its eight-foot-thick *2.4 m* walls topped by two remaining turrets. Other remains include the West Tower and parts of a defensive gateway. The original castle dates from the twelfth century, although there are remains of thirteenth- and sixteenth-century buildings. In 1644, during the Civil War, castle defenders held out for three months when it was besieged by Fairfax. Consequently it was 'slighted', which largely accounts for its ruined condition. It is ironic that thirteen years after the 'slighting', Fairfax's daughter Mary married into the family who owned the estate at the time of the seige, and the couple subsequently lived in the castle that Dad had knocked about!

On the attractive square stands a medieval market cross, and an ornate memorial to the Earl of Feversham. Bordering the square are some good hotels and inns. Part of the Feathers Hotel was a fifteenth-century cottage. The Black Swan (note that name is not displayed) includes the fine black-and-white-timbered Old Rectory.

All Saints Church includes twelfth- and thirteenth-century features, but is largely the result of Victorian rebuilding in 1849. Particularly fine is the Norman arch to the chancel. Fascinating wall paintings and windows are designed to illustrate the coming of Christianity to the area. Wooden panelling in the chancel is dedicated to the memory of the dead of the 22nd Dragoons. This armoured regiment was stationed at the camp which we passed on the way into Helmsley from August 1941 to February 1943. Formed in 1940, it was equipped with flail mine-sweeping tanks, and trained for one purpose only – the invasion of Europe. It was disbanded at the end of the war. Adze-worked panelling is by the famous Thompson of Kilburn, who identifies his work by discreetly positioned carved mice.

The great house in Duncombe Park was built in 1713. It is thought that the architect, Vanbrugh, had some influence on its design and siting. The park was described by Pevsner as 'one of the most extensive and bold landscaping exercises in England'. The terraces are famous for their views and temples, and were created at the same time as the terrace above Rievaulx. There are plans to open both house and park to the public in 1990.

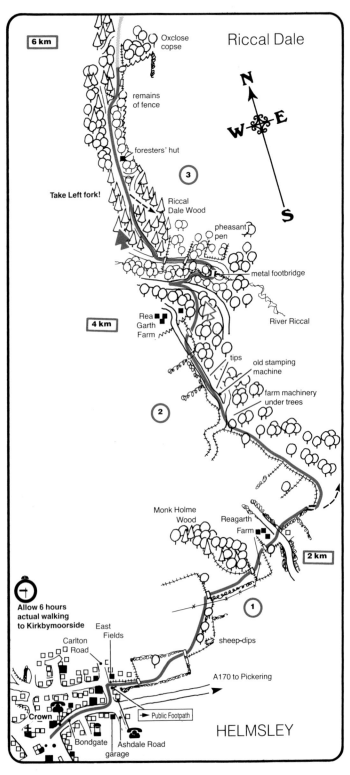

Riccal Dale

6 km

Oxclose copse

remains of fence

foresters' hut

③

Take Left fork!

Riccal Dale Wood

pheasant pen

metal footbridge

River Riccal

4 km

Rea Garth Farm

tips

old stamping machine

farm machinery under trees

②

Monk Holme Wood

Reagarth Farm

2 km

①

sheep-dips

Allow 6 hours actual walking to Kirkbymoorside

East Fields

Carlton Road

A170 to Pickering

Public Footpath

Crown

Bondgate

Ashdale Road

garage

HELMSLEY

42

Lunch: There is no lunch establishment on the way to Kirkbymoorside, so a packed lunch will be required. If you decide to linger in Helmsley to visit the castle *(open: 9.30),* then about picnic-time you will probably be in the region of the sheltered depressions of Pinderdale Howl and Howldale, just before the two miles *3 km* of rather exposed lane by Nawton Tower. On the other hand, the mill at Hold Caldron (four hours' walking) makes a very pleasant place for a break if you can defer food and rest until then!

Helmsley to Riccal Dale

Going: An easy field walk followed by a drop down into attractive, wooded Riccal Dale and a fairly steep ascent out.

In Ryedale Folk Museum at Hutton-le-Hole (page 51) there is a fine collection of flints and stone tools which were once used by early farming communities at Helmsley, indicating a considerable population here throughout the late Neolithic and Bronze Ages. Remains of a villa two miles *3 km* east of the town are proof of a Roman presence. William's Domesday Book gave the name Elmeslac and listed it as a modest village of thirteen families, two priests and a wooden church. The twelfth century saw the transformation of Helmsley into a prosperous small town, with the establishment here of the family of Walter L'Espec, which caused the castle to be built, and provided land for Rievaulx Abbey. In the eighteenth century, the town was an important centre in the flax linen industry, with a population of 3,000 and 26 alehouses to deal with the weavers' thirsts.

Some interesting publications on sale in the helpful Information Office on the Market Square give fuller details of the history of the town and the area.

Leave Helmsley market square along the Pickering road (Bondgate). Opposite petrol station, turn Left into Carlton Road and in few yards turn Right along signposted path just before East Fields. Through gate into field, and cross to gate in far Left corner. At sheep-dips on Right, path bears Left to fence. Through gate on Right to walk uphill, with hedge on Right. At tip of Monk Holme Wood through gate and bear Left to go through Reagarth Farm.

Garth comes from the Old Norwegian *garthr,* for enclosure.

Cross road and through gate to walk with hedge on Right to cross stile into Riccal Dale Wood. Turn Left to follow wood boundary. At collection of farm equipment and water troughs tucked under trees like military vehicles hiding from air surveillance, join and continue ahead on farm track to Rea Garth Farm.

Similarly named farm is just to keep the postman on his toes!

Through gate and just before farm, turn down Right through gate into wood and follow path steeply down to join forestry road, where turn Left. In few paces turn sharp Right onto green lane and cross River Riccal by impressive metal footbridge. Turn Left and follow wide track with river in trees on Left. Through *second* gate take grass track steeply up to Right.

Near top of climb, take Left fork and shortly pass foresters' hut on Right. Less than five minutes from the hut, fork up Right through remains of fence to walk with boundary wall and then Oxclose copse on Right.

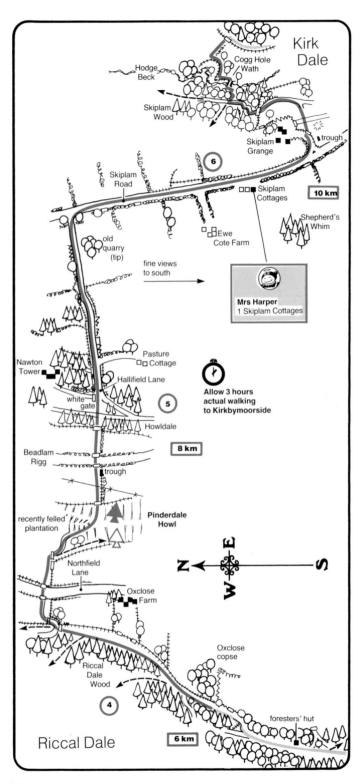

Kirk Dale

Cogg Hole Wath

Hodge Beck

Skiplam Wood

Skiplam Grange

trough

6

Skiplam Road

Skiplam Cottages

10 km

old quarry (tip)

Ewe Cote Farm

Shepherd's Whim

fine views to south

Mrs Harper
1 Skiplam Cottages

Pasture Cottage

Nawton Tower

Hallifield Lane

Allow 3 hours actual walking to Kirkbymoorside

white gate

Howldale

5

Beadlam Rigg

8 km

trough

recently felled plantation

Pinderdale Howl

Northfield Lane

N E S W

Oxclose Farm

Oxclose copse

Riccal Dale Wood

4

foresters' hut

Riccal Dale

6 km

Riccal Dale to Kirk Dale

Going: Very easy, level walking broken by dips into two interesting depressions. A long walk on a quiet, open lane is followed by a challenging stream crossing!

Continue along the top edge of Riccal Dale Wood and through gate onto hairpin bend of forestry road. Follow this Right, and cross field to Northfield Lane.

Look back Left for impressive view across tree-filled dale to Helmsley Bank, 1,076 feet *328 m.*

Cross lane and through gate into field to walk with fence on Right. Take the second of two gates and follow track down into Pinderdale Howl. Just beyond where second little valley comes in on Left, bear steeply up track, Left, to leave Pinderdale by gate and into field. With fence on Right, through gates to cross Beadlam Rigg lane and, at end of next field, down through firs into Howldale.

Howl comes from the Norwegian *hul,* for a dry valley. It is interesting that the names of Pinderdale Howl and the adjacent Howldale both include the Saxon *dale* and the Scandinavian *howl.*

Continue ahead to climb out of Howldale and join Hallifield Lane near white gate entrance to Nawton Tower.

A fine display of flowering shrubs can usually be seen in the boundary hedge of Nawton Tower on the Left. Over to the Right are distant views over flat cultivated land that was once Pickering Lake. This tremendous stretch of water was almost 30 miles *48 km* long and up to seven miles *11 km* wide, larger than any lake now existing in England. (Windermere, in the Lake District, is ten and a half miles *17 km* long and a mile *1.6 km* wide.) It was created by melt-waters from the thaw of the last Ice Age, 15,000 years ago. Huge glaciers which spread eastwards from Cumbria and south from Scotland combined with North Sea ice to surround the high moors, and trap melt-waters here along the northern edge of the Vale of York. The surface of the lake may have been 250 feet *76 m* above sea level.

Don't be perturbed that field boundaries here don't agree with your OS map. They have gone! This is 'cowboy' prairie land.

Follow lane to junction with Skiplam Road, where turn Right. After about fifteen minutes, turn Left into lane to Skiplam Grange. Before entering farmyard, turn Right through gate and bear Left down behind farm. Continue on sunken farm track, which in one place has been cut out of rock. Through gate to enter Skiplam Wood. After about four minutes on twisting, descending track, take thin path to Right which twists down to Hodge Beck and the ford at Cogg Hole Wath.

Wath is from the Norwegian *vasse,* for ford.

On the right of the ancient ford is a footbridge which would not be out of place in the Himalayas. Careful balance is required to negotiate the two long, pliable logs. A loose wire, probably intended as a hand rail, should be treated with circumspection.

Having survived the footbridge, turn Left to follow the fence by the stream. After a few yards through trees, turn Right to follow line of hawthorn bushes up field to gate into Mell Beck Wood. Through gate, turn Right along boundary track.

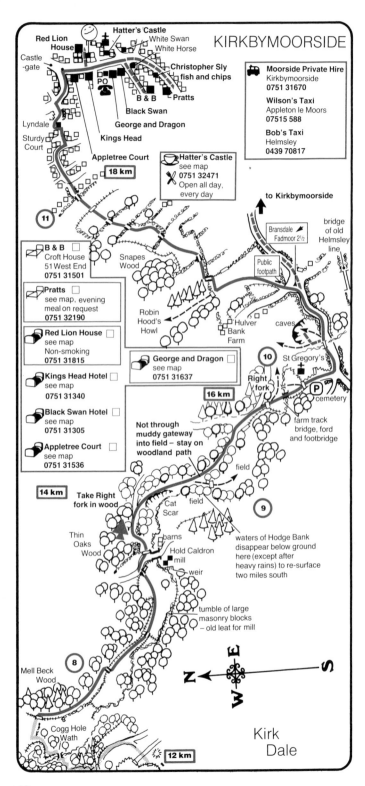

KIRKBYMOORSIDE

Red Lion House
Castle-gate
Hatter's Castle
White Swan
White Horse
Christopher Sly
fish and chips
PO
B & B
Pratts
Black Swan
Lyndale
George and Dragon
Sturdy Court
Kings Head
Appletree Court

18 km

11

🚗 Moorside Private Hire
Kirkbymoorside
0751 31670

Wilson's Taxi
Appleton le Moors
07515 588

Bob's Taxi
Helmsley
0439 70817

☕ **Hatter's Castle**
see map
🍴 0751 32471
Open all day,
every day

to Kirkbymoorside

Bransdale
Fadmoor 2½

bridge
of old
Helmsley
line

Public
footpath

🚜 **B & B**
Croft House
51 West End
0751 31501

Snapes Wood

🚜 **Pratts**
see map,
evening
meal on request
0751 32190

Robin
Hood's
Howl

Hulver
Bank
Farm

caves

Red Lion House
see map
Non-smoking
0751 31815

George and Dragon
see map
0751 31637

10

St Gregory's

Kings Head Hotel
see map
0751 31340

16 km

Right
fork

🅿
cemetery

Black Swan Hotel
see map
0751 31305

farm track
bridge, ford
and footbridge

Appletree Court
see map
0751 31536

**Not through
muddy gateway
into field – stay on
woodland path**

field

14 km **Take Right
fork in wood**

Cat
Scar

field

9

Thin
Oaks
Wood

barns

Hold Caldron
mill

weir

waters of Hodge Bank
disappear below ground
here (except after
heavy rains) to re-surface
two miles south

tumble of large
masonry blocks
– old leat for mill

8

Mell Beck
Wood

N E
W S

Cogg Hole
Wath

Kirk
Dale

12 km

Kirk Dale to Kirkbymoorside

Going: Pleasant woodland walking leads to old mill site and famous ancient church. Field walk into Kirkbymoorside.

Continue on track with field boundary on Right and Mell Beck Wood on Left. Shortly the path is diverted over stile on Right to continue in same direction in field. Over stile onto wide track to gate by mill bridge.

Over the bridge is Hold Caldron mill, now a private house.

Through gate by bridge into Thin Oaks Wood, and take Right fork to climb to viewpoint path on Cat Scar, high above Hodge Beck. Descend into wood where path leads to field gate, but take track forking Left through trees *before* reaching muddy gateway. This path wanders along just inside wood to emerge on wide grass track. In a few paces, take Right fork down through gate into field. Ahead to cross sometimes dry river-bed, by farm track bridge or footbridge. Through gate on Right of church.

Spend a few minutes in this delightful spot, where people have met to worship for nearly 2,000 years. The first St Gregory's Minster may have been the monastery that was founded in 654 by St Cedd, but the crypt at Lastingham (page 51) appears to have a stronger claim. In any event there was a church here in the seventh century, until it was destroyed by raiding Danes. It was rebuilt prior to the Norman Conquest. Of this church, only the nave remains, although masonry from the earlier church can still be seen. The church is famous for a Saxon sundial above the south door, beneath the porch. A cast copy is in the Science Museum, Kensington. An excellent booklet on sale in the church gives a translation of the sundial's inscription, which tells how the ruined early minster was 'all to brocan and to falan'. A service is held here every Sunday.

Past car park, turn Left on old Helmsley–Kirkbymoorside road to cross footbridge at ford. Immediately on Left is track to old quarry and famed Kirkdale Caves.

In the face of the quarry is an eight-foot-wide *2.4 m,* three-foot-high *1 m* entrance to a cave, from which have been recovered the bones of lions, bears, elephants, bison, rhinoceros and other animals. Discovered by quarry workmen in 1821, they were not identified until brought to the attention of a Dr William Buckland. The bones also included those of nearly 300 hyenas, and because of the small cave entrance, Buckland deduced that this was once the den of hyenas which had dragged in the remains of the various other animals. The bones are thought to date from about 70,000 BC. The cave divides into many channels, and there is a local story that a goose disappeared into the cave, only to reappear in Kirkbymoorside, our destination this evening. However you are not encouraged to look for this route – the goose arrived minus feathers!

Continue to crossroads. *(For those in an indecent hurry, the road ahead may be taken and you could be in Kirkbymoorside in fifteen minutes!)* Turn Left onto the Fadmoor road and immediately join footpath on Right to walk with fence on Left. Where fence ends, continue towards gate leading into Robin Hood's Howl, but instead of venturing into this overgrown valley, turn Right up to stile in corner and cross into field. Follow hedge on Right. Well-walked footpath past Snapes Wood enters Kirkbymoorside through a modern housing estate.

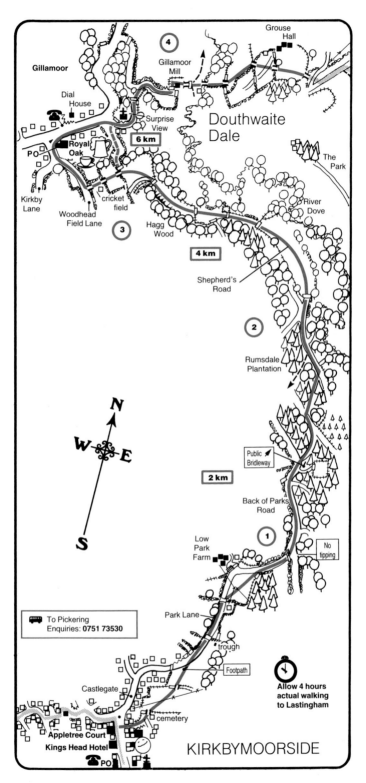

Gillamoor

④

Grouse Hall

Gillamoor Mill

Dial House ☎

✠ Surprise View

6 km

Douthwaite Dale

PO

Royal Oak

Kirkby Lane

cricket field

Woodhead Field Lane

③

Hagg Wood

The Park

River Dove

4 km

Shepherd's Road

②

Rumsdale Plantation

N
W ✦ E
S

Public Bridleway

2 km

Back of Parks Road

①

No tipping

Low Park Farm

🚌 To Pickering
Enquiries: **0751 73530**

Park Lane

trough

Footpath

🕐 Allow 4 hours actual walking to Lastingham

Castlegate

cemetery

Appletree Court
Kings Head Hotel

☎ PO

KIRKBYMOORSIDE

Lunch: The Royal Oak in Gillamoor opens for morning coffee, and does good lunchtime pub food. Pub lunches also available at the popular Crown in Hutton-le-Hole. Recommended Forge Tea Room in Hutton-le-Hole is open every day from May to October.

Kirkbymoorside to Douthwaite Dale

Going: A very pleasant walk along quiet lanes, through woodland, and along ancient field routes.

Kirkbymoorside – pronounced *Kirby* without the second 'k' – gets its name from 'church by the moor'. The busy Pickering-to-Helmsley road bypasses just to the south, leaving this a peaceful market-town. There have been two castles here, but these have both gone. A market is held on the cobbles in the main street every Wednesday. All Saints Church includes some Norman masonry, and a fifteenth-century roof and porch. Grooves each side of the doorway may be the result of sharpening arrow heads after morning service in readiness for compulsory archery practice. William Wordsworth and Mary 'sauntered about' the churchyard, while the coach-horses were fed, on the way home from their wedding at Brompton in 1802.

Leave Kirkbymoorside by passage in High Market Place, almost opposite Appletree Court. Follow round to Left and over stile into horse paddock and up to cross another stile and small field to turn Right on Park Lane. Still climbing, pass through two gates, with cottage on Right. Correct route leaves lane after second gate to cross field diagonally Right to rejoin Park Lane by conifer copse. At lane junction, turn Left onto farm track, impressively named Back of Parks Road. At Left bend, take wide green track into trees on Right, signposted Public Bridleway. Down to junction, where turn Left. Note fine view over young plantation. In a few yards, turn down thin overgrown track on Right to junction with wide track, where turn Left. Pass track down on Right and through gate ahead into field.

Follow pleasant grass track of Shepherd's Road, with tree-lined River Dove and The Park on Right and wood on Left. Through third gate into Hagg Wood and steeply up on once-paved sunken track. Emerge from wood by gate and leave track, which curves round to Left. Cross field diagonally and over stile in corner. (Gate on Right provides short-cut to church.) Cross small field and cricket field with hedge on Right, to turn Right on Woodhead Field Lane and Kirkby Lane. Turn Right on wide High Street of Gillamoor along to church.

Since the twelfth century the 'Surprise View' from the churchyard has been famous. The present church is largely nineteenth century. For many years the original dedication of the church was forgotten, but in 1927 it was reconsecrated to northern St Aidan.

Leave village by grass lane to Right of church, which bears Left below churchyard and drops down to join Gillamoor Mill lane. *This path is not a right-of-way, but Mr Johnson of Gillamoor has kindly given permission for users of this guide to walk this route. Please respect this privilege.* Turn Right on lane down to mill. Footpath passes to Left behind millhouse, crossing footbridges over mill leat and River Dove. Through two fields, with hedge on Right, and over stile into paddock in front of Grouse Hall to cross farm track, over stile and continue across next field to far Right corner to cross footbridge.

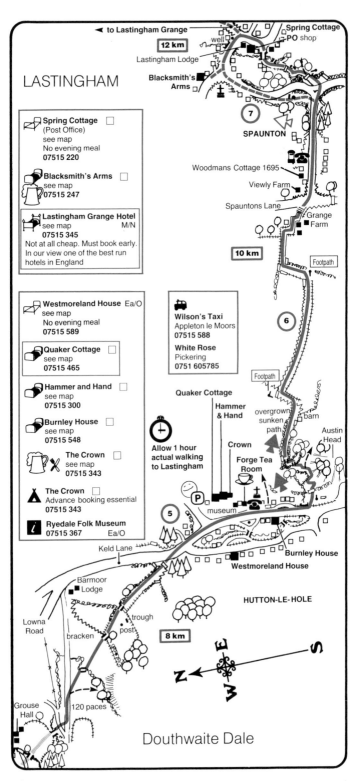

to Lastingham Grange

Spring Cottage
PO shop
well
12 km
Lastingham Lodge

LASTINGHAM

Blacksmith's
Arms

7

SPAUNTON

Spring Cottage
(Post Office)
see map
No evening meal
07515 220

Blacksmith's Arms
see map
07515 247

Lastingham Grange Hotel
see map   M/N
07515 345
Not at all cheap. Must book early.
In our view one of the best run
hotels in England

Woodmans Cottage 1695

Viewly Farm

Spauntons Lane

Grange
Farm

10 km   Footpath

Westmoreland House Ea/O
see map
No evening meal
07515 589

Quaker Cottage
see map
07515 465

Hammer and Hand
see map
07515 300

Burnley House
see map
07515 548

The Crown
see map
07515 343

The Crown
Advance booking essential
07515 343

Ryedale Folk Museum
07515 367   Ea/O

Wilson's Taxi
Appleton le Moors
07515 588

White Rose
Pickering
0751 605785

6

Footpath

Quaker Cottage

Hammer
& Hand

overgrown
sunken
path   barn

Austin
Head

Crown

Allow 1 hour
actual walking
to Lastingham

Forge Tea
Room

P

museum

5

Keld Lane

Burnley House

Westmoreland House

Barmoor
Lodge

HUTTON-LE-HOLE

Lowna
Road

trough

bracken   post

8 km

N E
W S

Grouse
Hall

120 paces

Douthwaite Dale

Douthwaite Dale to Lastingham

Going: Dalehead walk up into attractive village of Hutton-le-Hole, followed by climb up onto field paths on Tabular Hills and easy descent into Lastingham.

From corner of field footbridge, cross grass track and scramble up onto second wide grass track with fenced field on Right. Approximately 120 paces from where fence turns off to Right, take thin path to Right through bracken to junction of wall and fence below Barmoor Lodge. Over stile and continue with paddock boundary on Left. Stay on hedged track to Keld Lane and turn Right into Hutton-le-Hole.

This village, on the little rushing stream of Hutton Beck and with its wide, sheep-cropped greens, white-railed footbridges and neat cottages, is popular with photographers and artists. Do spend time in the excellent Ryedale Folk Museum near the Crown pub. Originally opened in a cottage in 1964, it has been greatly expanded to include a fascinating outdoor museum with buildings carefully moved from original sites to be re-erected and preserved here. These include two cruck houses, a manor-house, barns, a fully equipped blacksmith's shop, a saddler's, a wheelwright's, a glass-works and a foundry. Allow one hour, but you could easily spend two. *Open from March to October: 11.00 to 17.15 hrs. Admission charge.* Small church of St Chad contains furniture by the 'mice-man'.

At far end of village, by seat on green, turn Left on signposted footpath with Fairy Call Beck on Left. Through gate into field, keeping to Right to avoid boggy patch. Bear Right at *No Right of Way* sign and continue up below tree-covered slope of Austin Head on Right. In clearing, bear Left steeply up to stile and over into hedged lane to turn Left, then immediately over second stile and continue up overgrown sunken path to arrive, thankfully, on open, well-marked field paths.

Look back Left for fine views over Douthwaite Dale, and in the distance see again the TV aerial above Bilsdale.

Follow waymarks to pass through Grange farmyard onto Spauntons Lane, where turn Right and Left to walk along Spaunton's wide village street.

In the living-room of Manor House Farm, a Court Leet meets once a year to administer local common land.

Continue to road junction. *Brief detour can be made here to fine viewpoint marked by cross commemorating Diamond Jubilee of Queen Victoria in 1897, with a seat celebrating Queen Elizabeth II's 1952 Coronation. (Unofficial path drops down directly from cross to enter village near church.)* Back at junction, cross road to locate signposted footpath by gulley on Left. Follow attractive wooded path steeply down into Lastingham.

An interesting and attractive village, but best known for the unique crypt beneath St Mary's Church. It was here in AD 654, that St Cedd began building a monastery, but he died of plague before it was completed. His younger brother, St Chad, finished the work, but in the ninth century the monastery was destroyed in a raid by Danes. In 1078 an attempt was made to rebuild it, starting with this crypt in memory of St Cedd. It has remained virtually unchanged since. *Church history available.*

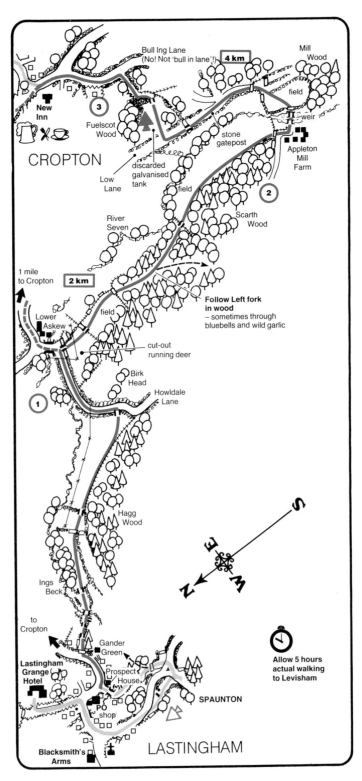

CROPTON

Bull Ing Lane
(No! Not 'bull in lane'!)

4 km

Mill Wood

field

New Inn

3

Fuelscot Wood

weir

Low Lane

discarded galvanised tank

stone gatepost

Appleton Mill Farm

field

2

River Seven

Scarth Wood

1 mile to Cropton

2 km

field

Follow Left fork in wood – sometimes through bluebells and wild garlic

Lower Askew

cut-out running deer

Birk Head

Howldale Lane

1

Hagg Wood

Ings Beck

to Cropton

Gander Green

Prospect House

Lastingham Grange Hotel

PO shop

SPAUNTON

S

E

W

N

Allow 5 hours actual walking to Levisham

Blacksmith's Arms

LASTINGHAM

52

Lunch: The excellent New Inn, Cropton may be too early for you (about two hours from Lastingham, three hours from Hutton-le-Hole). On the other hand you may think the friendly Swan Cottage, Newton-upon-Rawcliffe – open all day, except on Wednesday afternoons – is too late (four hours' walking from Lastingham and five hours from Hutton). Perhaps a packed lunch for a historic picnic at the Roman camps between the two?

Lastingham to Cropton

Going: A pleasant, level field and woodland walk to Appleton Mill. A steep little path leads easily up into Cropton.
Important: After heavy rain, the weir at Appleton Mill Farm may not be passable, and you should take the road from Lower Askew up into Cropton – about one mile 1.6 km.

Note the wisdom carved on the lintel of Lastingham Lodge on the corner. For 'hap' read 'chance' or 'luck'.

Leave Lastingham on Cropton road with bridge and Prospect House on Right. Immediately past last house on Right, Gander Green, take signposted footpath and over collection of stiles and footbridge into fields running parallel with Ings Beck, eventually walking with Hagg Wood boundary on Right. Over stile into Howldale Lane and turn Left with prominent Birk Head up on Right. Just before Lower Askew Farm *(see important note above about wet weather),* turn Right on signposted footpath to follow field boundary on Left. At end of second field go through gate into Scarth Wood, and in a few yards take Left fork to walk along top of tree-covered bank.

Over stile into field and continue with wood on Right. Through gate into Appleton Mill farmyard and follow farm road round to Left to cross duck-pond weir. Bear Left to far corner of field and Left through gate onto Low Lane. Ignore farm track bearing up to Right. About twenty-five paces beyond next gate, turn Right on thin track up small overgrown valley. Over stile at top to bear Left on hedged lane. At junction with Bull Ing Lane, turn Left to road and Cropton village.

Brewing beer at home was an offence in 1613, and it cost Henry Robinson four hours in the churchyard stocks here. Mike Lee of the New Inn is not likely to suffer that fate today. He brews two real beers on the premises: *Cropton Best* and *Cropton Strong.*

A walled enclosure in the High Street was once the village well-house, where water was hauled from a 300-foot-deep *91m* well. The hardware was reassembled in May 1988 after 68 years of disuse. Nearby St Gregory's Church has a twelfth-century font and a thirteenth-century south window. When I was last there, a sad little note complained that: 'The church mouse thrives on oasis blocks and electric cable. One day we will acquire an organ which plays only when asked.' Almost opposite the church, a cluster of dish aerials sprouts in a cottage garden. This is international earth station SCOLA 2, which is one of a world-wide chain of stations monitoring and recording foreign language material which is daily despatched to Creighton University, Nebraska. The remarkable John Standen, consultant to governments on satellite communications, hopes to set up a centre, open to the public, with multiple monitors, including one showing the Yorkshire Moors as seen from space!

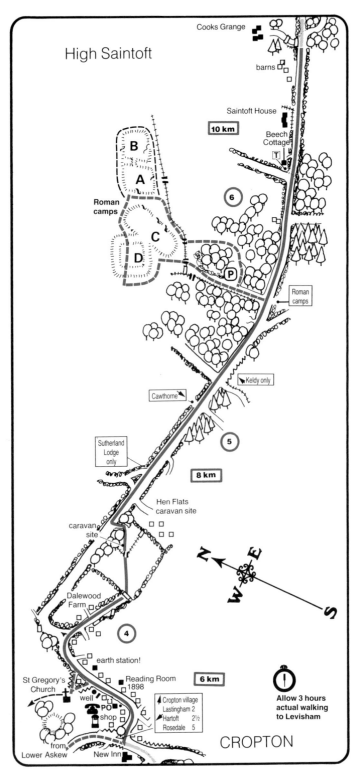

High Saintoft

Cooks Grange

barns

Saintoft House

10 km

Beech Cottage

⑥

Roman camps

B

A

C

D

ℙ

Roman camps

Keldy only

Cawthorne

⑤

Sutherland Lodge only

8 km

Hen Flats caravan site

caravan site

N
E
W
S

Dalewood Farm

④

earth station!

6 km

St Gregory's Church

Reading Room 1898

well

PO shop

▲ Cropton village
Lastingham 2
Hartoft 2½
Rosedale 5

Allow 3 hours
actual walking
to Levisham

from Lower Askew

New Inn

CROPTON

Cropton to High Saintoft

Going: Mostly road walking, but this gives you the opportunity to visit a remarkable Roman site. So press on uncomplaining, and enjoy the easy, relaxed walking – there are rewards not far away!

From the New Inn, bear Right to follow road through village. At Right bend at end of village, leave road for farm track past Dalewood Farm and through gate at end into field. Head for far Left corner, and cross stile into fenced caravan site and through copse onto road, where turn Right. After about ten minutes' walking, pass lane on Left to Keldy and continue for five more minutes to signposted entrance, on Left, to Roman camps. You are urged to include this visit in your Footpath Tour. *No admission charge.* Recommended routes round the camps have been waymarked, so walk to end of lane, passing car park, and over stile into site. Return to road after visit.

Here in the woods are the embankments and ditches of four separate defensive works attributed to the Romans. For many years there was speculation as to why they had needed to build such a large establishment, indicating a huge mass of troops. It was thought that the camp may have had something to do with the defence of the Roman road we will walk along tomorrow, but the size and actual siting were baffling.

Then, in the 1930s, the archaeologist, Sir Ian Richmond, conducted extensive excavations and came to a fascinating conclusion. This was a place where legionaries – the fighting-men of the army, and all with the status of Roman citizens – came to learn and practice the art of building camps. He was able to show that there were two separate occupations, or training exercises, separated by six to ten years – the date of the second being about AD 100. Each time, the camp-builders lived in one irregular-shaped, quickly erected camp, while they dug ditches and embankments, and erected wooden palisades on the adjacent camp to the recognised regulation pattern. Sir Ian identified these camps, as indicated on the map opposite. The occupants of camp C built A; whilst the occupants of B built D.

He also was able to determine that after the first 'training course', camp A was systematically demolished, although not completely finished. On the other hand, D was abandoned incomplete without demolition. It was concluded from the style of entrenchments in the 'living' camps, that no danger was expected, and no actual warfare was involved. Sir Ian also suggested that the first 'exercise' involved one or two cohorts from the Ninth Legion, based in York (a cohort was 480 soldiers), and the second, three cohorts.

The camps are thought to be unique, not only in Britain, but in the known Roman world, and the North York Moors National Park bought the site in 1983 to ensure their protection and make them available to the public. In addition to the waymarking, there are plans to install viewing platforms and explanatory boards, and eventually to produce literature.

Continue on road. In less than ten minutes of walking, the road turns Left at Beech Cottage, but continue ahead on cul-de-sac lane past Saintoft House to gates of Cooks Grange.

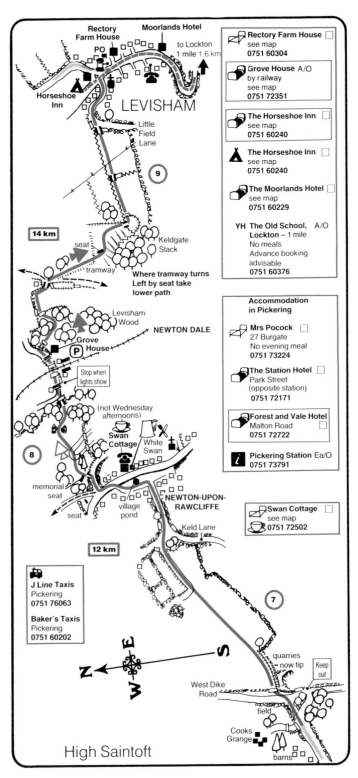

Rectory Farm House

Moorlands Hotel

to Lockton 1 mile 1.6 km

PO

Horseshoe Inn

LEVISHAM

Little Field Lane

9

14 km

seat

Keldgate Slack

tramway

Where tramway turns Left by seat take lower path

Levisham Wood

NEWTON DALE

Grove House

P

Stop when lights show

(not Wednesday afternoons)

Swan Cottage

White Swan

8

memorial seat

NEWTON-UPON-RAWCLIFFE

seat

village pond

Keld Lane

12 km

J Line Taxis
Pickering
0751 76063

Baker's Taxis
Pickering
0751 60202

N E S W

7

quarries – now tip

Keep out

West Dike Road

field

Cooks Grange

barns

High Saintoft

Rectory Farm House
see map
0751 60304

Grove House A/O
by railway
see map
0751 72351

The Horseshoe Inn
see map
0751 60240

The Horseshoe Inn
see map
0751 60240

The Moorlands Hotel
see map
0751 60229

YH **The Old School,** A/O
Lockton – 1 mile
No meals
Advance booking
advisable
0751 60376

Accommodation in Pickering

Mrs Pocock
27 Burgate
No evening meal
0751 73224

The Station Hotel
Park Street
(opposite station)
0751 72171

Forest and Vale Hotel
Malton Road
0751 72722

i **Pickering Station** Ea/O
0751 73791

Swan Cottage
see map
0751 72502

56

High Saintoft to Levisham

Going: A field walk into attractive Newton-upon-Rawcliffe, with a wonderful viewpoint over Newton Dale. Drop down into dale to cross restored North Yorkshire Moors Railway, and steeply up out of dale to Levisham.

At gates of Cooks Grange, where the remains of the road turns off to Right, continue on footpath ahead and climb up through undergrowth to West Dike Road. Turn Left on lane and immediately turn Right through gate into field to walk with fence, wall, hedge boundary on Right. Where this boundary ends, continue ahead. Over field crest, aim for small fields and farm track down on Left. At lane junction, turn Right and bear Left up lane into Newton-upon-Rawcliffe.

The wide single street has a well-populated duck-pond. Swan Cottage will serve you refreshments – and a bag of duck food!

Turn Left on green past pond and at end of village, by seat, turn Right on hedged lane which bears round to Right. Over stile by memorial seat.

The splendidly sited seat is dedicated to two cousins who served in the Royal Armoured Corps. One died 'somewhere in the Western Desert' in 1942, the other in Germany in 1944. Both were aged 21 years and both loved these moors.

The view from here is magnificent. Pickering Beck flows peacefully through the valley. However, 15,000 years ago the steep 400-foot *120 m* sides of Newton Dale gorge were being gouged out by a boiling torrent, as melt-waters from the Esk Valley thundered down to escape into Lake Pickering. When, in the 1830s, George Stephenson was commissioned to build a railway to link Pickering with Whitby, he ran a twelve-mile *18 km* section through this gorge, and one of the stations, Levisham, lies on our path below. At first the single line was horse-drawn, and half a mile *800 m* up the line to the Left stood Raindale Inn (now a field centre), which was a staging-post for the horses. In 1845, a second track was laid, and steam-engines appeared. If you have timed your arrival right, you might be lucky enough to be treated to the sounds, sight and smell of a steam-hauled train. The line was closed in 1965, but was mercifully taken over by railway enthusiasts and is now one of the best-loved restored lines in the country. A few years ago it became 'Melton Carbury' for BBC television's *Brideshead Revisited*. *See note, over, about a rail excursion to Pickering.*

From memorial seat, drop down to cross hairpin-bend lane. Locate sunken track in gorse by aiming midway between two railway signals in distance. Path bears down Right, through trees, to cross footbridge and railway line.
Watch for train warning lights!
Immediately past Grove House hotel, turn Right on signposted footpath, over footbridge, and through gate into Levisham Wood. Follow path up through wood and through gate into field. Continue up field with hedge on Left. At barn, turn Right to join grassed line of old tramway, which rises straight and steep. Where tramway bears Left at seat, drop down to take a lower path which bears Left, then up Right, to stile in wall above trees in Keldgate Slack. Cross stile and turn Left. Follow wall on Left to enter Levisham near church.

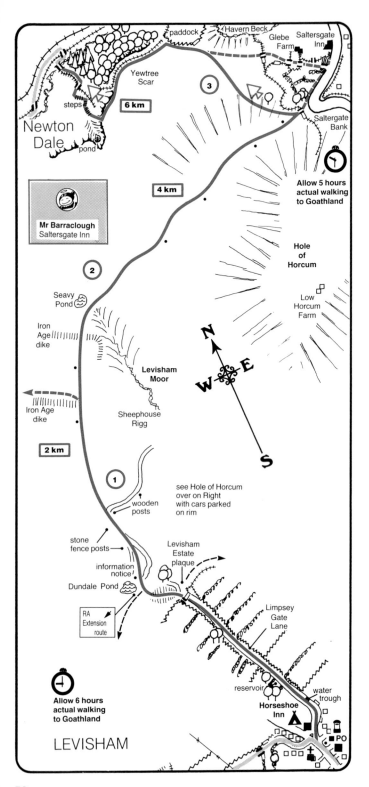

Havern Beck

paddock

Glebe Farm

Saltersgate Inn

Yewtree Scar

(3)

6 km

steps

Newton Dale

pond

Saltergate Bank

Allow 5 hours actual walking to Goathland

4 km

Mr Barraclough
Saltersgate Inn

(2)

Seavy Pond

Iron Age dike

Hole of Horcum

Low Horcum Farm

N

W · E

S

Levisham Moor

Iron Age dike

Sheephouse Rigg

2 km

(1)

wooden posts

see Hole of Horcum over on Right with cars parked on rim

stone fence posts

information notice

Dundale Pond

RA Extension route

Levisham Estate plaque

Limpsey Gate Lane

reservoir

water trough

Horseshoe Inn

Allow 6 hours actual walking to Goathland

PO

LEVISHAM

58

Lunch: The historic Saltersgate Inn is only an hour and a half away, so is more practical for morning coffee than lunch! It looks like a picnic lunch again, and an attractive spot is by Wheeldale Bridge at the beginning of the Roman road.

Levisham to Newton Dale

Going: A pleasant, airy moorland path to the famous depression of the Hole of Horcum, a coffee-stop in a famous pub, and an attractive walk down into Newton Dale.

Leave the pleasant, wide street of Levisham along Limpsey Gate Lane, with Horseshoe Inn on Left. Through gate onto Levisham Moor to follow well-walked track ahead, passing Dundale Pond on the Left. After about fifteen minutes' walking, see notice about an Iron Age dike on the Left.

If visibility good, make detour along ancient earthwork to viewpoint two minutes away to look down again into Newton Dale.

Perched on the escarpment, Left, is Skelton Tower, which was built in 1850 by the Rev. Skelton of Levisham. Although said to be a shooting-lodge, locals claim it was a place for a quiet drink!

Pass on the Left another ancient dike and Seavy Pond. Path now follows along rim of the great Hole of Horcum.

The hole is three-quarters of a mile *1.2 km* across and 400 feet *120 m* deep, and is the result of thousands of years of erosion by springs – old legends blame the giant, Wade! Ahead are the three 160-foot-high *49 m* domes of Fylingdales Ballistic Missile Early Warning Station. Built in the 1960s, these familiar landmarks will soon be replaced by pyramids.

Come to a fence and stile at the hairpin bend of the A169 Whitby-to-Pickering road. *If you propose visiting the Saltersgate Inn, cross stile and turn Left to walk down grass verge of this busy road. Rejoin route by footpath just before inn, and pass in front of Glebe Farm. Follow edge of deep tributary valley of Havern Beck to gate of small walled paddock.*

The isolated Saltersgate Inn has a peat fire burning which has been kept alight since 1801! The pub name comes from the days of the Salt Tax. Fish caught on the coast was brought here to be salted with 'smuggled salt'. Landlord, John Barraclough, will point out the tiny window in line with a sharp bend in the road at Saltergate Bank, where a look-out could give warnings of approaching excise men. Ask him too about the ghost, and the body under the ever-lit fire!

If you decide against the hospitality of the inn, do not cross stile, but turn Left to follow fence on your Right. Where this begins to drop sharply down to fields on the Right, continue on track ahead, which gradually passes down the hillside and crosses to gate of small walled paddock.

Do not enter paddock, but bear Left to follow wall on Right. At an angle, the boundary changes to a fence running along Yewtree Scar, the rim of tree-filled Newton Dale. At obvious deep rocky cleft take first steeply descending track. Fortunately track soon becomes well-constructed steps, which take you easily down, past firs on Right, to footbridge over Pickering Beck in the bottom of the dale. Cross stile to walk with fence and beck on Left, and railway line on the Right only a few feet above your head!

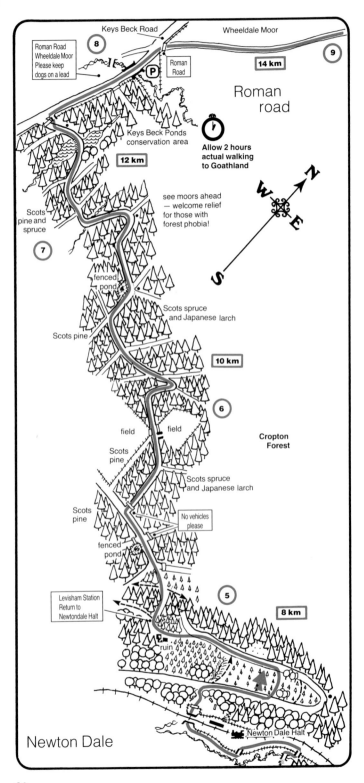

Newton Dale to Roman road

Going: Forestry roads and tracks cross from east to west of Cropton Forest. Easy and mainly level, but rather a lot of trees. A pleasure to get back onto open moorland and join the remains of the Roman road leading over Wheeldale Moor.

In a few yards cross stile in fence to continue with fence on Right. Bear Right under railway bridge at Newton Dale Halt station on the North Yorkshire Moors Railway.

This 'request-stop' was opened in 1981 to provide access for walkers to a network of forest paths. Newton Dale was part of the Normans' great Royal Hunting Forest of Pickering until the thirteenth century. In the fourteenth century, iron was worked on the Levisham side of the dale, and trees were felled to provide the necessary charcoal. In the nineteenth century there were cattle- and sheep-farms here. In 1919, after a German submarine blockade highlighted Britain's dependence on timber, the Forestry Commission was formed. In 1928 the dale became one of the Commission's first properties, and over 5,000 acres have now been planted.

Cross station parking area to join forestry road, where turn Right. There is an unofficial track, opposite the station exit, which runs up by the stream and Yaul Sike Slack. However the Forestry Commission would prefer you to walk for about three minutes along the forestry road to the Right where, at a copse, a waymarked track goes steeply up to another copse on the top road. On this top road turn Left. After about eight minutes' walking, where the forestry road bears Right, continue ahead on a thin, and sometimes muddy, track which passes ruin on the Left.

This was once Beulah House, a farm now fallen into disrepair.

Past the ruin, the path bears Right to climb up among the firs of Cropton Forest. Discount paths to Right and Left and continue up to a junction of forestry roads, part of a Forest Drive. Continue straight ahead on this drive. Over gated cross-roads by fenced pond, and take next road on Right, signposted *No vehicles please.* Stay on this metalled (and sometimes dusty!) forestry road with all its twists and turns, ignoring all un-metalled openings and tracks.

After about an hour of easy walking on this same road, pass the conservation area of Keys Beck Ponds. Leave forest at last, to turn Right onto Keys Beck Road. Pass Wheeldale Beck car park and picnic site, and at fence bear Right to leave road, and through gate onto Roman road.

Perhaps the greatest and most lasting legacy that the Romans left us was the remains of their 10,000-mile *16,000 km* road network. After they went, it was not until the eighteenth and nineteenth centuries that we rediscovered how to build roads to match them. They were engineered, like the camps at Cropton, by legionaries, and usually consisted of side gutters, drainage channels, and a raised embankment or 'agger' up to 20 feet *6m* wide. Upon this would be built foundations of stone, clay and sand, depending upon the local materials available. A top surface would consist of cobbles, or rammed sand and gravel. Of this 16-foot-wide *5 m* Roman road, the top surface has been eroded by centuries of northern weather, and only foundation stones and drainage channels remain.

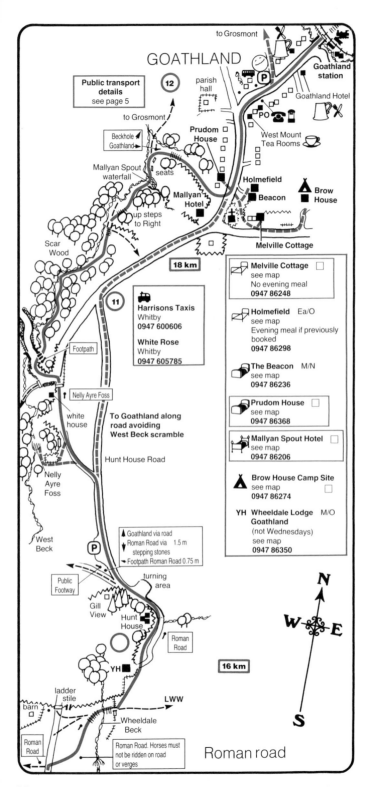

To Grosmont

GOATHLAND

Goathland station

12

Public transport details
see page 5

parish hall

Goathland Hotel

to Grosmont

Beckhole ◄
Goathland ►

Prudom House

PO

West Mount Tea Rooms

Mallyan Spout waterfall

seats

Holmefield

Beacon

Brow House

up steps to Right

Mallyan Hotel

Melville Cottage

Scar Wood

18 km

11

Harrisons Taxis
Whitby
0947 600606

White Rose
Whitby
0947 605785

Footpath

Nelly Ayre Foss

white house

To Goathland along road avoiding West Beck scramble

Nelly Ayre Foss

Hunt House Road

West Beck

P

Public Footway

Gill View

Hunt House

Roman Road

YH

16 km

ladder stile

barn

LWW

Wheeldale Beck

Roman Road

Roman Road. Horses must not be ridden on road or verges

Roman road

▲ Goathland via road
▼ Roman Road via   1.5 m
   stepping stones
→ Footpath Roman Road 0.75 m

turning area

Melville Cottage ☐
see map
No evening meal
0947 86248

Holmefield Ea/O
see map
Evening meal if previously booked
0947 86298

The Beacon M/N
see map
0947 86236

Prudom House ☐
see map
0947 86368

Mallyan Spout Hotel ☐
see map
0947 86206

Brow House Camp Site ☐
see map
0947 86274

YH **Wheeldale Lodge** M/O
Goathland
(not Wednesdays)
see map
0947 86350

N
W E
S

Roman road to Goathland

Going: From the Roman road there is the choice of an easy walk along an open lane into Goathland, providing a last look at the moors, or an attractive path along West Beck with two waterfalls. The latter involves a bit of scrambling in places, so in wet weather, when rocks are slippery, it may be prudent to stick to the lane – but if, at this stage of the walk, you are skipping about with all the confidence of a young gazelle, go for West Beck and good luck!

No one appears to be certain when the Romans built this road or where it went. A popular theory is that it was constructed over 200 years after the Cropton camp exercises, when the Picts and Scots were presenting an ever-increasing threat and extra troops were moved to the north. A series of look-out posts and signal stations were hurriedly built along this coast, and it is thought that this military road was built from Malton *(Derventio)* to serve these stations – probably including the one still to be seen at Kettle Ness, eleven miles *18 km* due north of here. Let your imagination repair the surface of the road as it weaves through the heather, and there again are the legionaries, marching, wearily and warily, to ward off the day when this part of the crumbling Roman empire would finally be abandoned.

After about ten minutes' walking on the Roman road, at the Ministry of Works sign on Left, take track down on Right past notice forbidding horse-riding. At bottom, cross stepping-stones over Wheeldale Beck and over stile, and bear Left while our old friend, the Lyke Wake Walk, continues ahead up to Simon Howe. Pass in front of Wheeldale Lodge Youth Hostel and follow wall on Left round to Hunt House. Continue past car park on road. After less than five minutes' walking, come to a footpath sign pointing down to Left. Continue for a few yards to wide grass track on Left. *Alternatively continue ahead on the road and be in Goathland in less than half an hour!*

Turn down grass track. *Just before fenced paddock, bear Left with fence on Right, to make a detour to visit the Nelly Ayre Foss – not the most exciting of waterfalls, but a pretty spot.* Back on the track, continue with wall on Left. Where wall turns down to Left, continue ahead to white house, through gate and onto road, where turn down Left. Follow road round to Right and cross stile before bridge over West Beck. Follow attractive, but sometimes tricky, path along by beck. Shortly after crossing stile in wall, take steps up to Right. This path shortly returns to the beck, just before Mallyan Spout. Beyond this impressive 70-foot *21 m* waterfall, and past two seats, take signposted footpath up to Right. Join road by Mallyan Spout Hotel and other accommodation.

Opposite is St Mary's Church (1896), built on the site of an 1150 hermitage. This may be the right place to spend a minute or two at the end of your North York Moors adventure. (You might even locate the six mice left by wood-carver, Thompson of Kilburn!)

For Goathland station, on North York Moors Railway, turn Left on road for less than fifteen minutes' walk through village. Much recommended three-mile *5 km* walk to Grosmont, via delightful Beck Hole (see page 3), leaves the village car park.

That's it. Well done! I hope you enjoyed it.

Symbols

———	*Footpath-Touring* route	accommodation, not cheap
– – – –	*Footpath-Touring* alternative route	pub
- - ➤	other paths	recommended pub
✔	signposts	licensed
+++++	fence	snacks
∧∧∧∧	wall	meals
⌒⌒⌒⌒	hedge	□ open all year
⊂▭⊃	gate	*M/O* open March to October, etc.
⌗ ⌗	stile	specially recommended
⊸∫ ⌐	bridge	recommended start time showing time to allow for walk
～	stream	telephone
⩟	boggy	letterbox
▲	steeply up	taxi
△	steeply down	bus
—×—×—	overhead lines	information
♧♧♧	trees, deciduous	castle
♠♠♠	trees, coniferous	ⓟ car park
△	trig point	toilets
✝	church	Guardian Angel
□	building	camping
■	building mentioned in text	BS boundary stone
★ ★	cairns	FB footbridge
⑧	miles from overnight stop	NT National Trust
16 km	kilometres from overnight stop	PO post office
	accommodation, economy	WM waymark
	accommodation, medium	YH youth hostel

Thanks

I am most grateful for help from many people in determining this *Footpath-Touring* route. Particular thanks to Harry Mead, author of *Inside the North York Moors*, for his interest and interest. Thanks also to the staff of North York Moors National Park, North Yorkshire County Council, the Forestry Commission and the various estate offices and individuals who have kindly made concessions for users of this guidebook.